D1109536

# ─ *On Snooker* ─

# — *On Snooker* —

*The Game and the Characters Who Play It*

*Mordecai Richler*

The Lyons Press

Guilford, Connecticut
An Imprint of The Globe Pequot Press

The Lyons Press is an imprint of the Globe Pequot Press.

Printed in The United States of America

10 9 8 7 6 5 4 3 2 1

Design by A Good Thing, Inc.

*Library of Congress Cataloging-in-Publication Data*
Richler, Mordecai, 1931–
    On Snooker / Mordecai Richler
        p. cm.
    ISBN 1-58574-179-5
        1. Snooker—Anecdotes. I. title
GV900.S6 R53 2001
794.7'35—dc21

2001029612

*For Max, Poppy, and Simone*

*Playing snooker gives you firm hands and helps to build up character. It is an ideal recreation for nuns.*

ARCHBISHOP LUIGI BARBARITO

*Man is a gaming animal. He must always be trying to get the better in something or other.*

CHARLES LAMB

*To use a cue at billiards well is like using a pencil, or a German flute, or a small-sword—you cannot master any one of these implements at first, and it is only by repeated study and perseverance, joined to a natural taste, that a man can excel in the handling of either.*

WILLIAM MAKEPEACE THACKERAY

# — *On Snooker* —

CLIVE EVERTON, snookerdom's Rashi, once pronounced on two of the game's stalwarts, Cliff Thorburn and Kirk Stevens, both Canadian born and bred, declaring them long-standing chums. "Stevens was a mere twelve-year-old," wrote the affable Everton in the monthly journal *Snooker Scene*, "when he painstakingly accrued four dollars with which to challenge Thorburn, a superstar even then, in 1970, *in the subculture from which Canadian snooker had not even begun to emerge.*" (Emphasis mine.)

A small-time hustler in that "subculture" back in the late forties, I took Everton's observation as an ad hominem snub of my heritage.

Games have always played an important role in my life, culminating in my becoming a novelist, a rogue's game wherein I was at last empowered to make my own rules, rewarding and punishing as I ordained. Submitting to book tours enriched by probing TV interviews: "Is this book of yours, Mordy, based on fact, or is it just something you made up in your own head?"

To begin with, I was captivated by the simplest of childhood games common to Canadian street kids in the early forties: bolo, yo-yo, flip-the-diddle, and such beginner's card games as fish and casino. And at the age of ten I was already an impassioned fan of Montreal's Club de Hockey Canadiens, *nos glorieux*, and our Triple "A" baseball Royals, as well as the weekly Gillette-sponsored fight broadcasts out of Madison Square Garden in New York, the big time.

I came to snooker at the age of thirteen, in 1944, my first year at Baron Byng High School in Montreal. Montreal has a confessional-school system and BBHS operated under the aegis of the city's Protestant School Board. But squatting as the school did on St. Urbain Street, in the heart of the working-class Jewish quarter, the brown brick building as charming as a Victorian workhouse, the student body was 99 percent Jewish. We were a rough-and-ready lot. The sons and daughters of pants pressers, sewing-machine operators, scrap metal dealers, taxi drivers, keepers of street-corner newsagent kiosks, plumbers, shoe-repair mavens, and grocery store proprietors. My mother didn't trust Klein, the corner grocer, who would pass off yesterday's kümmel bread as today's when it should have been reduced from ten to eight cents a loaf. "He never stops bragging about his son the doctor. Some doctor. He has that stutter, you could die before he gets a word out. He married for money and he does abortions."

She took the jolly French Canadian coal-delivery man for a crook as well. "He has to serve Jews it just about kills him. You go round the back and count the bags he dumps in the shed. I paid for twelve. Twelve *full* bags."

The ladies' auxiliary of the Young Israel Synagogue was another problem. "I would be president, if only I was married to a dentist like Gloria Hoffer, big deal, she doesn't know he plays around with his receptionist, would I say a word? But your father is a junk dealer, he comes home he sits down to supper in his Penman's underwear, what if somebody nice rang the doorbell, I ask you?"

Before he sat down my exhausted father would wash his hands with Snap, but he never succeeded in getting out all the grit. It was embedded in his fingernails and the cuts in his calloused hands. He would read the New York *Daily Mirror* or *News* at the kitchen table with the linoleum cloth, beginning with Walter Winchell, wetting a thumb before turning a page. When he was finished, I was able to catch up on Alley Oop, Dick Tracy, Maggie and Jiggs, Red Ryder, Li'l Abner, and Ella Cinders. Sometimes Macy's famous department store ran brassiere ads, and I would take the newspaper with me into the bathroom.

Round the corner from Baron Byng, on St. Laurence Boulevard (The Main, in Montreal parlance), lay the Rachel Pool Hall, my deliverance from classes in geometry and intermediate algebra, both of which confounded me. Beginning snooker players at the Rachel were obliged to apprentice on the last of four tables, lest we miscue and rip the baize cloth. The faded baize on the humiliating last table no longer mattered. It had already been mended here and there with black tape. There were sticky Coca-Cola stains and cigarette burns. Imitating the more seasoned players, I learned to select a number of cues from the wall rack, ostentatiously rolling them on the table until I settled on one that wasn't hopelessly warped. If my opponent managed a difficult pot, I would bang my cue butt three times on the floor, just like the other Rachel habitués. However, much to my chagrin, I never achieved star status, my very own cue locked into the wall rack like the one that belonged to the all but unbeatable Izzy Halprin, who also pitched for the YMHA Intermediates and would go on to serve on one of those rusty tubs sailing out of Naples, laden with concentration camp survivors, that ran the British blockade of Palestine. Another player, Mendy Perlman, a name to conjure with in those days, became a lawyer, sadly misunderstood, obliged to spend time in the slammer when it turned out that too many aged widows had left him money in the wills he had prepared for them. Before being sentenced, Mendy, once Baron Byng's knockout debater, gave the judge what for. "Six million weren't enough for you," he hollered. "So today you got yourself another victim. Congratulations."

I had to be satisfied with eventually qualifying for the first table, a rite of passage second only to the much earlier test of Jack and Moe's barbershop on the corner of Park Avenue and Laurier, later displaced by a Greek loan society.

To begin with, our obdurate mothers, notorious nontippers, escorted us to Jack and Moe's for our twenty-five-cent brushcuts. A degrading plank was slipped through the silvery arms of the old-fashioned chair so that neither barber had to stoop to mow our hair. They got through the job as quickly as possible, because the presence of our unsmiling mothers, knitting needles clicking away (knit one, purl two), meant the barbers couldn't exchange the latest dirty jokes with the men in the other chairs.

The barbershop plank was not the only ignominy I suffered in those early days. If I refused to eat my lukewarm breakfast porridge, or declined my large morning spoonful of cod-liver oil, my irate mother would reach for the wall phone. Ordering the party line we shared the connection with to ring off immediately, as this was an emergency, she would pretend to dial Eaton's department store, saying, "I want to exchange my bad little boy for a nice girl."

Then, one absolutely magical afternoon, I was allowed to venture unescorted into the barbershop, and Jack or Moe no longer had to slide that plank through the arms of the chair to cope with me. I had not only sprouted sufficiently tall but, O happy days, I was now considered a fit audience for dirty jokes.

"How does a mink get babes?"

"You got me, Moe."

"The same way a babe gets mink."

Qualifying for table number one in the Rachel was one thing, but getting there in time to claim it was something else again. It meant hurrying to the poolroom as soon as classes were out, the race to the swift, until my bunch and I hit on a solution. If we sneaked out of school before the last class of the day, there was seldom a problem. Cutting afternoon classes altogether was even better. Financing our truancy at twenty cents a game was no hardship, as patriotic aunts and uncles would often give us twenty-five-cent stamps toward our War Savings Certificates. Sixteen stamps, worth four dollars, were required to complete a certificate that could be redeemed for five bucks five years later. However, Mr. Freed, who ran the cubbyhole hot-dog emporium adjoining Baron Byng, would buy our stamps for twenty cents each, and also offered a deal on streetcar tickets. The boss of the Rachel, a stout Serb, took our interests to heart. When he knew we were playing hooky he stood guard by the front window, and if he saw one of our schoolmasters approaching he would call out a warning, and eight of us would scramble, squeezing together in the stinky little toilet until the menace had passed. In that situation the guy to watch out for was fat, pimply Nat Ginsberg, who specialized in silent farts. Nat, incidentally, has turned out surprisingly well. Last time I ran into him he was wearing dark designer sunglasses, an Armani suit, and Gucci loafers. He's big in something to do with computers and told me that he employs a personal trainer. He offered me a lift home in his BMW, a cellular phone clapped to his ear for the ride as, with a vintner's catalogue open on his steering wheel, he continued to bid on a wine auction in New York.

Pool tables were also available here and there in our neighborhood. However, while we considered such a crude game simply dandy for American ruffians, it was unacceptable to St. Urbain Street sports like us. Pool is for bangers. Played on a ridiculously small table with outsize pockets that beckon rather than reject a less than accurately aimed pot. A pool table measures a risible $4\frac{1}{2}$ feet by 9 feet, while a regulation snooker table is 6 feet by 12 feet. Checkers cannot be compared to chess, nor pool to snooker, a far more subtle game wherein tactical skills count for as much as potting ability.

If I zigzagged between Baron Byng and our cold-water flat after school was out, a seven-block hike even if I avoided the Rachel, I had to run a gauntlet of two other poolrooms: the Mount Royal Billiards Academy, where we could sometimes watch a real pro, "Atomic" Eddy Agha, practice, and the Laurier. So I seldom got home before six p.m.

"Where were you?" my mother would demand, her manner indignant. "I'm sitting here afraid to use the phone in case you've been run over by a car or got into another fight with those French kids, rickets is too good for them, and Bessie is waiting for me to call her with my marble cake recipe, as if she won't ruin it no matter what I tell her."

"Why, that anti-Semite, Mr. Hoover, made me stay in after classes."

"He should be reported to the authorities."

"Things will only get worse if we make trouble."

I went on to enjoy a brief, only fitfully successful stint as a teenage poolroom hustler. Frequenting snooker venues where I was unknown, I would sit on the bench and feign amazement at the pots made by older players—say, guys in their twenties. "Wow!" I'd exclaim, slapping my cheek. "Hey, you're a real pro." Finally I'd ask, "Could I play you, mister?"

"Only if you've got a buck, kid."

"Jeez. A buck. Okay, but only once."

If I won, which wasn't always the case, it would go to another game for double or nothing. I usually thought it politic to quit once I was ahead four bucks. However, a couple of times, maybe more, I risked going for a whopping eight bucks before skedaddling.

"Hey, come on. Where in hell do you think you're going, you little bastard?"

"I mustn't be late for shul. I have to say kaddish for my mother."

In my halcyon days as a poolroom bum, the worst temptations to sin we faced in the Laurier came from itinerant peddlers, old geezers lugging cardboard suitcases, who offered cut-rate prices on guaranteed 100 percent leather wallets fallen off the back of a truck, and who also dealt in neckties featuring bare-bosomed cuties in hula skirts. Oh, and there was the smelly creep with the disconcerting facial twitch who sold playing cards, imported from Gay Paree, that displayed nude couples or threesomes on the backs, some of them in positions yet undreamed of by my bunch, that made us giggle nervously. *Holy cow, would we be expected to do that one day?* Not so long as we married nice Jewish girls, said my older cousin Baruch. Most of the men making out on the playing cards were starkers except for black silk socks held up by garters, for all we knew *de rigueur* in Gay Paree.

If the Laurier was marginally tainted by the intrusion of a

thieving peddler or a small-time pornographer, who rather than arousing us scared the hell out of my bunch, we were usually redeemed, come five o'clock, by the invasion of a wash of students from the nearby Merchaz ha'Torah Yeshiva. The rabbis did not object to their presence in the Laurier. They welcomed it as a convenience. Whenever they required three or four bodies to make up a minyan, the ten men needed for a religious service, they knew exactly where to round them up.

Horny teenagers in those days, we dreaded the coming of Saturday nights. Our angst, such as it was, struck us as we quit school on Friday afternoons, loping home to work the phones, once or twice even daring to dial the number of Molly Spivack, who was to die for. The agonizing question was, would we manage to get a date for Saturday night, or would we be humiliated again?

We were sixteen-year-olds at the time, grade eleven students at Baron Byng, and the ungrateful girls we had invested in so beneficently for years—treating them to double features at the Rialto followed by toasted tomato-and-mayo sandwiches, washed down with a Coke or milkshake, at Ben Ash's—raining dimes on the nickelodeon to get them in the mood—had suddenly forsaken us. Upwardly mobile in their nifty sweaters, advertising their concupiscence, tricked out in tight skirts, nylons, and high heels, they now preferred the company of older guys who were already studying at McGill. Pretentious pricks in those red-and-white sweaters embossed with a big M, who could dangle the keys of Daddy's car at our former girlfriends. Getting up to only God knows what hanky-panky, parked on some dimly lit cul-de-sac. It drove us crazy.

This being our sad plight, we often had to put up with being men without women, as Mr. Hemingway had it, on Saturday nights, settling for endless sessions of snooker at Park Avenue Billiards.

Most people I know can remember exactly where they were on the day John Kennedy was assassinated. Or whom they were with when Neil Armstrong landed on the moon. Me, I can also recall the sweet spring Saturday night in Park Avenue Billiards when I cleared all the colored balls off the green baize in one inspired turn at the table, amazing me as well as Hershey Tannenbaum, my stunned opponent.

Footloose in Paris in 1950, I suffered fits of deprivation, unable to find a snooker table anywhere on the Rive Gauche, but I did manage to work in the odd game of billiards in the back room of a Boulevard Saint-Germain café, with Sinbad Vail, the editor of *Points*. Sinbad paid me ten dollars for my first published short story, which led me to abandon poolroom hustling for a more profitable life in the world of letters.

Later, in London, where my wife, Florence, and I were rooted for some twenty vintage years, I was able to shoot the occasional game of snooker with my friend Ted Kotcheff, upstairs in the Bale of Hay, on Haverstock Hill, the pub where Henry Cooper used to train.

We returned to Montreal in 1972 with our five children and, shortly afterward, I strolled through my old neighborhood, only to discover that the Rachel, the Mount Royal Billiards Academy, and the Laurier were all gone. Laurier had been transmogrified into an elegant French Canadian boulevard, trendy boutiques and restaurants displacing kosher butchers, the bicycle-repair shop, the Chinese laundry, and the Italian hatblocker-cum-shoeshine parlor. Gone was Schacter's Cigar & Soda, where my bullied father, fearful of his own father and his wife as well, not one of his penny mining stocks a winner, used to retreat to the back room two nights a week for gin rummy games at half a cent a point. Also no longer in business was the store where our mothers could add to their collections of odd cups and saucers, or acquire tchotchkes for mantelpiece display (say, three clay see-no-evil, hear-no-evil, speak-no-evil monkeys), and table lamps with porcelain Madame du Barry bases, the lampshades themselves protected by cellophane that our mothers never peeled off lest the shades collect dust. A piece essential to just about every St. Urbain Street parlor in those days was a replica of Rodin's *The Thinker*, which, unlike the dreaded poolrooms, was meant to inspire the children. Poolrooms were okay for our Shabbos goy, the saucy Irish kid who lit our Sabbath fire for ten cents and was going nowhere, but not for Jewish boys with a future. You've got a poolroom, as Robert Preston would later belt out in *The Music Man*, and you've got trouble with a capital T.

A couple of years after we returned to Montreal, I sneaked a snooker scene into my screenplay for *The Apprenticeship of Duddy Kravitz*. Richard Dreyfuss, who had never held a cue before, astonished director Ted Kotcheff by making a nifty pot in a first take when it was called for in the script. Faithful to my addiction, I also wrote snooker scenes for James Woods and Alan Arkin into the screenplay for another novel of mine, *Joshua Then and Now.*

We acquired a cottage on the shores of Lake Memphremagog, in Quebec's Eastern Townships, in the mid-seventies, and there I realized a lifelong fantasy, my very own snooker table. Working with a local contractor, Florence designed a room that could be annexed to our dacha. It measured the required twenty-four feet by eighteen feet, allowing ample spare space for cue play while accommodating a regulation-size table. A marvel to behold.

If, as the fastidious Clive Everton had it, the "sub-cultural" snooker venues of Canada tend to be sleazy and smoke-filled, our room qualifies as an arcadian dream come true. It sits on a bluff, the surround of huge picture windows overlooking a stand of birch and maple and ash and pine trees and the still waters of Lake Memphremagog. A placard, a gift from my son Daniel that has proven invaluable in settling disputes, is mounted in the room. Across the top it reads:

SNOOKER

The Rules of the Game

Authorized by the Billiards Association

and Control Council

A group photograph of the 1986 Oxford University Ice Hockey Team, including our son Noah (who earned only a half blue for his efforts, hockey being a colonial sport), hangs on the same wall as a photograph of another player of distinction in his prime: Maurice "The Rocket" Richard. On a different wall of this sports museum of a sort, featuring my heroes, there hang portraits of Tom "The Black" Molineaux and the great Daniel Mendoza, both assuming their ring stance.

Tom Molineaux came to England from America in 1810 "and found himself," wrote Pierce Egan in his classic *Boxiana*, a book first published in 1818, "in the most enviable capital in the world, LONDON—a perfect stranger, a rude, unsophisticated being, who, resting upon his pugilistic pretensions to excellence, offered himself to the notice of the public, the patron of those gymnastic sports, which, from their practice and support, have instilled those principles of valour into her hardy sons, producing exploits by land and sea, that have not only added greatness, but given stability to the English character."

The Virginia-born Molineaux, a former slave who briefly laid claim to the heavyweight crown, lost his title to Tom Cribb at Thisleton Gap, Leicester, on December 18, 1877, before a crowd of twenty-five thousand.

Daniel Mendoza was the first of a pride of Jewish boxers in England that included "Dutch Sam" Elias, the Belasco brothers Aby and Issy, "Star of the East" Barney Aaron, Ikey Pig, Bernard Levy, and Moses Levy, a.k.a. "Ugly Baruk." Contemporary observer George Barrow claimed that "it is these that have planted rottenness in the core of pugilism, for they are Jews, and, true to their kind, have only base lucre in view. . . ."

Much as it pains me, I am honor bound to admit that Barrow had a point. In *Prizefighting: The Age of Regency Boximania*, John Ford quotes an account of an 1801 fight between the splendid Jew Isaac Bitton, and Paddington Jones:

". . . while sitting on his second's knee, [Bitton] felt for the 1s. 6d. that he had put into his drawers, previous to the battle; not finding it, he refused to continue till he had searched for the same. Mendoza (his second) was quite enraged at this stupid conduct, and urged that the time was expired, but all his entreaties were in vain, till Bitton felt the money near one of his knees, when he resumed the fight and proved the conqueror."

However, my trusty *Encyclopedia of Jews in Sport*, by Bernard Postal, Jesse Silver, and Roy Silver, has it that Daniel Mendoza, born July 5, 1764, in Aldgate, was not only the first of his faith to become heavyweight champion (1792–95), but also "the father of scientific boxing and the man whose fists helped to stem a vicious tide of anti-Semitism in England." Not universally, clearly, for when his arch-rival "Gentleman Dick" Humphries defeated him before a large crowd in 1788 he proclaimed, "I have done the Jew." But, ho ho ho, when the done Jew met Humphries again in 1789 he thrashed him in fifty-two minutes. A year later Mendoza required only fifteen minutes to dispose of Humphries yet again.

Pierce Egan, that incomparable observer of the sweet science, wrote of Mendoza's triumph over Humphries in *Boxiana*:

Mendoza in conquering so noble and distinguished a

competitor added considerable fame to his pugilistic achievements; but the greatest merit attached to the conquest was the manner in which it was obtained.

Prejudice so frequently distorts the mind, that unfortunately, good actions are passed over without even common respect; more especially when they appear in any person who may chance to be of a different country, persuasion, or colour; Mendoza, being a Jew, did not stand in so favourable a point of view, respecting the wishes of the multitude towards his success, as his brave opponent. . . . But truth rises superior to all things, and the humanity of Mendoza was conspicuous throughout the fight— often was it witnessed that he threw up his arms when he might have put in a most tremendous blow upon his exhausted adversary. . . .

Once my snooker table was in place in our dacha, I inaugurated the annual Boxing Day Richler Cup Tournament, an event not yet recognized by the snobs who run the World Professional Billiards and Snooker Association. Competitors in the tournament, which was an all-day (and then some) jubilee during the years we spent Christmas on the lake, included our three sons, Daniel most proficient with the cue; a number of their friends; and the working stiffs who were my late-afternoon good companions at the Owl's Nest, an unassuming watering hole perched on cinder blocks on Highway 242: Sweet Pea, Coz, Dipstick, and Buzz.

I must say that giving up the Townships for winters in London, as Florence and I did in 1993 when we acquired a flat in Chelsea, has deprived us of a number of social-cum-cultural events, among them the annual Wild Game Dinner at the Owl's Nest.

The Owl's Nest banquet was not for vegans. Tables were laden with wild turkey. Deer livers sizzled in pans, while porcupine, gray squirrel, and black bear bubbled in cauldrons (coyote was eschewed for being too chewy). These delicacies were washed down with quarts of Molson's Ex and a brand of Ontario vino that could, at a pinch, clear car windshields of frost. Smoking, bawdy language, and sexual harassment were encouraged, but "wacky-tobaccy" was not tolerated.

In the absence of a string quartet, the management provided a fiddler, screechy beyond compare, or somebody who could master the battered piano with the six missing keys. This long, enchanted evening usually culminated in one of the celebrants breaking a chair over the head of a neighbor, his hollered explanation charged with baffling sexual contradictions, as in, "You've been screwing my woman, you fucking little faggot!"

True, London has its compensations. Even its attractions. At dinner parties there, for instance, I have never had to cope with plastic cutlery, as we did at the Wild Game Dinner. But I miss my Townships companions, especially Big Foot. Big Foot wintered in a remote shack high in the hills, but once a week he descended through the snowdrifts to the bar. Attired in a shiny black suit and soiled white shirt with a ruffled collar, sporting an enormous jeweled crucifix in lieu of a necktie, he would sit down at a table and order three quarts of Molson's Ex. Then he would bet anybody a dollar that he could lift him off the floor by his trouser belt "wiff my teef." One week Big Foot failed to appear, so a bunch of regulars piled into a four-wheel drive laden with cases of beer, and headed for the hills. A distraught Big Foot was discovered staring into space at his kitchen table. "My wife must be very angry wiff me," he said. "She hasn't spoken wiff me for two nights. I can't get her out of bed."

One of the regulars slipped into the bedroom to investigate and returned to tell Big Foot, "She ain't angry with you. She's dead."

"Oh, so that's it," said Big Foot, enormously relieved.

Each contestant in our Boxing Day Tournament anted up a $10 entry fee, the winner entitled to a purse of $150, match play and beer consumption beginning at ten a.m. We would break at one for Florence's superb chili con carne and then play would resume, often continuing into the early morning hours. I must admit that our competition differed in at least one respect from world championship play at the Crucible Theatre in Sheffield. In that pressure cooker, play tends to go up a notch or two come the finals, but in our case it deteriorated.

To this day, whenever I'm enduring a bummer of a morning at my typewriter in my upstairs studio, I slip down to bang the balls around on the green baize. Baize, as defined by Dr. Johnson in his dictionary, is "A kind of coarse open cloth stuff, having a long nap, frized on one side, and sometimes not frized, according to the uses it is intended for. The stuff is without wale, being wrought on a loom with two treddles, like flannel. *Chambers.*"

Potting a difficult red, I pretend I'm taking on any one of those Crucible hotshots, giving him what for:

CONSTERNATION AT CRUCIBLE
500-1 Outsider, Sprung from Canadian Sub-Culture,
Dazzles Spectators with His Play.

## — *2* —

IN 1993 Florence and I acquired a flat in "the most enviable capital in the world, LONDON," where we hunkered down for the winter months, never returning to Lake Memphremagog before the first of May. This enabled me to watch, on TV, Stephen Hendry perform at the Crucible, his play mesmerizing. Hendry, who looks much younger than his thirty-one years, bears the burden of being acknowledged the best professional snooker player ever by the game's cognoscenti. But on occasion he could drive me crazy, falling behind by a seemingly insurmountable number of frames until—responding to my loud cries of dismay, I like to think—he would suddenly shift into top gear and take the next ten frames, effortlessly sinking ostensibly impossible long shots, demoralizing his opponent. Challenged, Hendry usually soared to perfection, his cue action incomparably graceful.

A frame, I should point out, ends when all the balls have been potted—snooker for sunk—or, as is more often the case, when one player has accumulated a number of points that far exceeds what is still available on the table, and his opponent concedes. A snooker player has to think at least four shots ahead. After sinking a red, his cue ball must roll to a stop at precisely the right angle for him to take on a colored ball, preferably the black, which yields the most points. Should his cue ball stop three inches short or, stroked too hard, run two inches too far, it could undermine what promised to be a frame-winning clearance of a hundred points or more—that is to say, a century.

The 1999 Embassy World Championship at the Crucible Theatre had to be accounted the most grueling Hendry had ever entered, as well as a risky business for me, too, as I took him for my talisman. If he won, it would be for the seventh time, a modern-day record, and I would be rewarded with a fruitful summer at my typewriter. A formidable trial for Hendry, but also an ordeal for me. One hundred hours of white-knuckle afternoon and evening TV, spread over seventeen days. I settled into my sofa to watch, lining up my traditional pacifiers on the glass-topped coffee table: a ten-pack of Davidoff's Demi-Tasse cigarillos, a plentiful supply of cashews, a bowl of cherry tomatoes, a bottle of the Macallan and another of Highland Spring mineral water—the latter a gesture of support for Hendry, who sports the Highland Spring logo over the breast pocket of his waistcoat.

In the opening round, Hendry required ten frames to win, immediately falling behind 0-2 to Paul Hunter, winner of the 1998 Welsh Open. *Goddamn it, Stephen, wake up!* Irritatingly down 8-7, Hendry did rally to prevail over the next three frames. In the press conference that followed, he said, "It's a massively important win for me because I couldn't have faced another fortnight at home when I knew I should be here. In the words of Steve Davis, they'll have to scrape me off the table. I feel I'm getting stronger and stronger."

Hendry's second opponent, James Wattana of Thailand, managed to hold Hendry to a 7-7 tie before he began to slide. In the nineteenth frame, Hendry threatened to secure an amazing sixth maximum clearance of 147 points, having potted the first ten reds with blacks. In order to chalk up a maximum—rare, but not quite as rare as a no-hitter in baseball—a player must pot all fifteen reds followed by blacks, and then the six colored balls in their proper sequence. Unfortunately Hendry faltered on his eleventh red. Bridging awkwardly over a cluster of reds, he inadvertently grazed the pink with his cue. A foul. But then, far from flustered, he carried on to eliminate Wattana 13-7.

Next up in the quarter-finals was Matthew Stevens, a twenty-two-year-old accountant's son, whom Hendry quickly disposed of 13-5.

Taking advantage of a two-day break before Hendry met the immensely talented but troubled and often underperforming Ronnie O'Sullivan, I was able to squeeze in some work, as well as renew my supplies of cherry tomatoes and cashews. Writing in *Snooker Scene,* Clive Everton, the pre-eminent critic of the game, described this contest as one of the classic matches in Crucible history: "in terms of pure quality its finest session. It was one of those rare contests in which both players were seen at the peak of their powers."

It began with Hendry putting together breaks of 126, 82, and 86, quickly building a 3-0 lead without O'Sullivan potting a ball. He led 6-2 at the end of the first eight-frame session. But in the second session, on the following day, a revived, suddenly inspired O'Sullivan cut Hendry's lead to 10-7, and went on from there to pull into a 10-10 tie. In the next frame, O'Sullivan potted fifteen reds with blacks, and the colors up to the blue, but lost his chance for a 147, never mind the £167,000 bonus that went with it, when the pink got caught in the jaws of a far pocket. After twenty-five frames O'Sullivan led for the first time in the match, 13-12, and then Hendry rallied to take the next four frames and win 17-13.

The engaging Mark Williams, survivor of an exhausting fortnight, was Hendry's opponent in the finals, the first prize worth £230,000. All the pressure would be on Hendry, whom some observers had written off as past it after he had been humiliated 9-0 in the first round of the U.K. Championship six months earlier. "That night I never thought I'd challenge for a title again," said Hendry, "let alone be a realistic contender at the Crucible."

Hendry also had a jinx to deal with. Williams, six years his junior, had already defeated Hendry in the 1997 British Open, the 1998 Benson & Hedges Masters, and the 1999 Welsh Open. But Hendry was never in trouble in the final, taking the title, his record seventh, 18-11. "I was in the doldrums for so long," he said afterward, "to come out on the other side like this gives me huge satisfaction." He promised to return the next season to win as many titles as possible. "My game is back to the level I expect it to be and my old confidence has come flooding back."

MY *Encyclopedia of Jews in Sport* pulls no punches when it comes to chastising Gentile interlopers, possibly on the time-honored principle that if you let one come in they will all want to join. Take, for example, the case of Max "Madcap Maxie" Baer, world heavyweight boxing champion, 1934–35. True, his paternal grandfather was a Jew from Alsace-Lorraine, but his father was not a practicing Jew and his mother was of Scotch–Irish descent. "Despite this," the encyclopedia notes with a certain asperity, "Max did wear a Magen David on his trunks and proclaimed himself a Jew. However, many believe this was merely for publicity purposes."

On the other hand, the encyclopedia is generous in celebrating even my coreligionists of dubious achievement. The baseball entry for Hyman "Hy" Cohen reads: "Pitcher, b. Jan. 29, 1931 in Brooklyn, N.Y. Played for Chicago Cubs in 1955. Total Games: 1. Pitching record: 0-0."

Unique among sports compendiums, the encyclopedia includes a section on chess, but there are no entries whatsoever for snooker or pool. This is irksome, considering that there are entries for both table tennis and polo, the latter section largely given over, as you might expect, to commemorating the feats of five Rothschild barons.

By way of compensation, two pages are devoted to the accomplishments of my brethren in billiards. John Kling, born in Kansas City in 1875, became a baseball catcher of some distinction, playing with the Chicago Cubs 1900–08, and going on from there to win the world professional billiards championship in 1909, the year in which he was a baseball holdout.

Another Jew, John Brunswick, born in Switzerland in 1819, emigrated to the U.S. in 1886. After putting in time as an errand boy, an apprentice carriage maker, and a steward on an Ohio River steamer, he founded his own carriage manufacturing plant in Cincinnati in 1845, and built what has been described as the "first perfect billiard table in the United States." Fourteen years later an American billiard championship was held, and over the next three decades the game became America's leading participant sport. And of course Brunswick tables and cues are still popular on both sides of the Atlantic.

Dr. Johnson was scornful of "balliards" in his dictionary, dismissing it as "A play in which a ball is driven by the end of a stick; now corruptly called *billiards*." In his *Dictionary of Accepted Ideas*, Flaubert sarcastically described billiards as "A noble game. Indispensable in the country." The *Oxford English Dictionary* defines billiards as "A game played with small solid ivory balls on a rectangular table having a smooth cloth-covered horizontal surface, the balls being driven about, according to the rules of the game, by means of long tapered sticks called cues." I plucked this definition from my 1961 edition of the *OED*, and have since sent them a letter, composed in my most pedantic style, reminding the editors that ivory balls have not been in use in professional tournaments since 1926.

The *OED* attributes first usage to Spenser, 1591: "With all the thriftless games that may be found. . . . With dice, cards, with billiards." It also quotes Shakespeare, from *Antony and Cleopatra,* 1606: "Let it alone, let's to billiards," which suggests that Will wrote fast and lacked an editor who would have pounced on such an anachronism. *Bartlett's Familiar Quotations* yields no reference to snooker and but one to billiards, from Gilbert and Sullivan's *The Mikado*:

> On a cloth untrue,
> With twisted cue
> And elliptical billiard balls!

But Clifton Fadiman's *Book of Anecdotes* proffers the most famous and enduring quote about the game, this from the British philosopher and economist Herbert Spencer (1820–1903):

"Spencer was playing billiards with a subaltern who was a highly proficient player. In a game of fifty up Spencer gave a miss in balk and his opponent made a run of fifty in his first inning. The frustrated philosopher remarked, 'A certain dexterity in games of skill argues a well-balanced mind, but such dexterity as you have shown is evidence, I fear, of a misspent youth.'"

Mary Queen of Scots was allowed to play billiards during her incarceration, and when that privilege was revoked she wrote a stinger of a letter to the Archbishop of Glasgow to complain. Such was Mary's devotion to the game that when she was beheaded her doctor, obviously a sentimental fellow, removed the green baize from the billiards table and wrapped her body in it. Another doomed royal, Marie Antoinette, was also an enthusiast. Louis XIV was fond of the game, and by the mid-eighteenth century it was being played from palaces in Russia to taverns in America. Mozart, according to report, was such an avid player that he often retired from scribbling tunes to bat the balls about. In 1846, Pope Pius IX had a billiard table installed in the Vatican. Tennis aside, it was the only sport officially tolerated in the Holy City.

The origins of billiards, from which the far more popular game of snooker evolved, are in dispute. One account traces billiards back to the sixth century B.C., its source the Scythian philosopher Anacharsis, who claimed to have witnessed a game similar to it while traveling in Greece. Others, who maintain that the game was played by ancient Greeks and Romans, were nicely—dare I say it?—snookered by the French economist Jacques Bonhomme. In 1885 he ventured that, had billiards been a Roman diversion, Horace would assuredly have devoted an ode to it, and Nero would have been distracted from his famed incendiary exploit by so agreeable a pastime.

England, China, Italy, and Spain all claim to have invented the game. What is known beyond doubt is that the French writer Clément Marot, who died in 1544, mentioned the game in one of his poems. The first description of billiards in English appeared in Charles Cotton's *Compleat Gamester* in 1674, and George Chapman, in 1598, has a character say, "Go, Aspasia, send for some ladies who could play with you at chess, at billiards, and other games."

According to Eric Partridge's *Origins*, the word "billiards" is derived from the French *billard*, or *billart*, meaning staff, hence a cue, from *bille*. *The Dictionary of Word Origins*, by John Ayto, adds that "the cue is the clue to the word's history, for it comes from French *bille* 'tree trunk,' hence 'long cylindrical bit of wood,'" but he also allows that the "import of the *-ard* suffix is not altogether clear."

In a bit of a stretch, Victor Stein and Paul Rubino, joint authors of the opulent *The Billiard Encyclopedia: An Illustrated History of the Sport*, would have us believe that the game has its roots in an ancient Egyptian bat and ball ceremony. In support of their thesis they reproduce a photograph of a relief from the temple of Deir el Bahari, showing Thothmosis III stepping up to the plate, as it were, in a symbolic bat and ball ceremony in the year 1500 B.C. If that's what he's doing, it could be argued that the ancient slugger was also the forefather of baseball, cricket, and, for that matter, ice hockey as well.

"The question of who invented billiards in Europe is pointless, however," wrote Messrs Stein and Rubino, "as billiards was not invented in Europe at all, only named there," imported by the French Knights Templar, the only lasting benefit of the Crusades.

In *Billiards without a Master*, published in 1850, Michael Phelan wrote:

> Billiards is a game of French invention, the word itself derived from the French word Bille, signifying ball.
>
> With regard to its first coming to notice, authorities differ. By some, it is supposed to have been first played by the Romans about the time of the Consul Lucullus; and by others to have been introduced by the Emperor Caligula—at all events, if known to the ancients, it was probably lost at the downfall of the Roman Empire, or else preserved by the monks of succeeding ages, and revived again at a later date.
>
> Its first appearance was immediately after the first Crusade, when it was introduced by the Knights Templar. The members of that refined and intelligent Order most probably obtained their knowledge of the game at the Court of the Comneni, at Constantinople, the seat of the Roman Empire of the East.
>
> With the downfall of that Order, caused by the jealousy of their superior wealth, intelligence and refinement, the game fell into disuse, and though probably practiced by a few, was not again revived till the reign

of Louis XI of France. That unwarlike, though able and politic prince was passionately fond of the game, and it was soon adopted by the courtiers of that monarch, and practiced by the ladies of the court.

It became more widely known in the reign of Henry III, one of his successors, and was styled by that luxurious monarch, the "Noble Game of Billiards." The game was so fascinating that it spread over Germany, Spain, Italy, and England.

Snooker, a rib torn from billiards' side, did not emerge full-blown but evolved through a forerunner—with a possible tip of the hat to Thothmosis III—called pyramids, in which fifteen red balls were initially placed in a triangle, the apex of the pyramid set in what would become snooker's pink-ball spot. Next in evolution came a game called life pool, wherein each player was given a cue ball, and each time an opponent's object ball was potted by a player, the opponent lost a life and some money as well. Three lives lost and a player had to fork out supplementary boodle, and when that was forfeit he was a goner. The last survivor was entitled to all the dibs in the poke. Finally the black ball, which would become the most coveted one in snooker, was introduced into a game called, appropriately enough, black pool.

Black pool was favored by the officers of the Devonshire Regiment stationed at Jubbulpore, in India. Then, lo and behold, one day in 1875 a young subaltern, later Colonel Sir Neville Chamberlain, introduced a variant game, as yet unnamed, into the officers' mess. It called for fifteen red balls and one each of yellow, green, brown, blue, pink, and black. Each time a player potted a red, he next took on a colored ball, replaced on the table if potted. Once all the reds had been accounted for, the yellow, green, brown, blue, pink, and black had to be potted in sequence. When Chamberlain moved on to the hill station in Ootacamund, after he was wounded in the Afghan war, the game caught on at the Ooty Club, where the billiards room remains a shrine to this day.

I am indebted to Clive Everton's *Embassy Book of World Snooker* for an account of that elegant venue, written by Trevor Fishlock when he was the India correspondent of the London *Times:*

> The room itself is entered through a door properly fit- ted with a peephole, marked "Wait for stroke," so that you do not in ungentlemanly fashion cause distress at the table. The room has ceiling beams and white walls hung with the skulls and heads of nineteen beasts and with large pictures of the Defence of Rorke's Drift, the retreat from Moscow, the battle of Tele-Kebir and the Charge of the Light Brigade. It has a handsome table over which, if you are fortunate, you may be permitted to lean and sight your cue almost as a sign of obeisance. The room's furnishings are redolent of leisured snookery evenings, joshing and cigar smoke, as the balls click, spin, and glide across the faded baize. On the wall near the cue rack there are framed accounts and letters testifying to the origin of the game and its curious name.

In an interview with Compton MacKenzie in 1938, Chamberlain explained that the game had got its name when it was discovered that a first-year cadet at the Royal Military Academy, Woolwich, was dubbed a "snooker"—that is to say, the lowest of the low, snooker being a corruption of *neux,* the French for "cadet." "The term was new to me," said Chamberlain, "but I soon had the opportunity of exploiting it when one of our party failed to hold a coloured ball which was close to the corner pocket. 'Why, you're a regular snooker.'

"I had to explain to the company the definition of the word, and to soothe the feelings of the culprit I added that we were all, so to speak, snookers at the game, so it would be very appropriate to call the game snooker. The suggestion was adopted with enthusiasm and the game has been called snooker ever since."

According to the *OED,* which obviously does not credit Chamberlain's tale, the word "snooker" is of obscure origin. However, Everton notes that Chamberlain's claim to have invented the game is supported by a number of imposing military chaps, among them Major-General W. A. Watson, Colonel of the Central Indian Horse, Major-General Sir John Hanbury-Williams, Sir Walter Lawrence, and Field Marshal Lord Birdwood. Birdwood remembered the peripatetic Chamberlain, just possibly the godfather of all poolroom hustlers, introducing the game into the mess of the 2nd Lancers at Bangalore. On the other hand, there is evidence that Chamberlain merely transported a game already in place in London into India. A notice of the rules for

"Savile and Garrick Snooker," dated 1869, still hangs in the Garrick, and included is a saucy rule that reads, "In the event of the yellow ball being involved in a foul stroke, it is the custom of watchers to cry out the word 'Bollocks.'" In the same room there hangs an 1869 painting by Henry O'Neil, RA, that shows a large number of club members, including Anthony Trollope, watching an early form of snooker, possibly life pool.

In the 1880s snooker was taken up by the Maharajah of Jaipur, a true sport who chartered a troop of elephants to transport tables to his castle. He appointed John Roberts Jr., a British billiards champion who became an early advocate of snooker, Court Billiards Player for Life, providing him and his wife with a hundred servants and an annual stipend of £500 to fill the office of teacher and exhibition player. Snooker balls were then made of ivory, which would result in the slaughter, over the years, of an estimated twelve thousand elephants.

"The ivory brought from the island of Ceylon," wrote Michael Phelan in *The Game of Billiards*, published in 1859, "is the best that can be used for billiard balls, the tusks being far more solid than those from Africa, less friable than those from Continental Asia, and more classic in proportion to their density than any other." However, even the high-quality ivory torn from the elephants of Ceylon presented problems. Only one out of every fifty tusks was sufficiently clear-grained to make a billiard or snooker ball. To pass muster, a ball had to be cut from the center of the tusk, soaked in water, and seasoned for up to two years before carving. This made those ivory balls, as Phelan noted, dreadfully dear: ". . . if any inventive genius would discover a substitute for ivory, possessing those qualities which make it valuable to the billiard player, he would make a handsome fortune for himself, and earn our sincere gratitude. . . ." As well, I imagine, as an enthusiastic blast of trumpets from the surviving elephants of Ceylon. With innovation in mind, Phelan—a partner in Phelan & Collender, a firm that had, by the 1860s, become America's largest billiard suppliers—began to run newspaper advertisements across the country offering $10,000 in gold to any "inventive genius" who created a substitute billiard ball.

First past the post was John Wesley Hyatt, a twenty-eight-year-old journeyman printer out of Albany, New York. Improvising in a small shack behind his house in the best Tom Edison tradition, he made a billiard ball of sorts by compressing odd bits of cloth, wood, and paper into spheres, adding glues, shellacs, and resins for binders. In 1865 he filed for a U.S. patent, number 50,529, for an imitation billiard ball molded from "layers of muslin or linen cloth coated with shellac or ivory dust." Alas, these first artificial balls failed to yield the satisfying click that the real stuff rendered when caroming off each other on the green baize. So Hyatt, working with his older brother Isaiah, went back to work, and in 1868 the enterprising pair had a lucky accident that led to the discovery of celluloid. No small matter. For this, wrote Stephen Fenichell in *Plastic: The Making of a Synthetic Century,* "launched phase one of the Plastic Age: moldable, malleable, protean by nature."

The mishap, so to speak, came about when John Wesley inadvertently tipped over a bottle of printer's cuticle, which congealed into a length of transparent film. "Gazing down at this sturdy slice of hardened film," wrote Fenichell, "it occurred to Hyatt that a billiard ball coated with such a compound might display the elusive properties he was looking for." So in April 1869 Hyatt applied for U.S. patent 88,634 for "an improved method of coating billiard balls by dipping them in a solution of colored collodion."

Hyatt dispatched samples of his collodion-coated billiard balls to a number of select poolrooms, asking them to conduct trials. However, being a responsible fellow, he did warn his field-testers that the highly nitrated collodion coating was a chemical kin to volatile guncotton, and therefore careful as you go, gents, as "a lighted cigar if applied to the ball, would at once result in a serious flame." Not only that, but "any violent contact between the balls" would invariably "set off a mild explosion, like a percussion guncap," obviously adding a certain fillip to the game. One of Hyatt's volunteers, a saloonkeeper in Colorado, wrote the inventor that he didn't mind, but every time the balls collided, "every man in the room pulled a gun." A *New York Times* wag wrote, "No man can play billiards with any real satisfaction if he knows that his billiard balls may explode in a series of closely connected explosions, thereby spoiling a promising run and burying players under the wreck of tables and cues."

Then, in 1909, eureka! A millionaire entrepreneur, Leo Baekeland, who was a member of the Chemists' Club in New

York, invented Bakelite, which didn't burn, with elasticity, he justifiably claimed, "approaching that of ivory." In 1912 Hyatt, acknowledging the inevitable, instructed his Albany Billiard Ball Company to eschew celluloid for Bakelite.

Finally, in another refinement, there was a switch to a substance called Crystalate, and then to the Super Crystalate balls. The latter substance was introduced when supplies of crushed cow's shinbones—used in the manufacture of Crystalate—dried up. The crushed shinbones used to be passed on to ball manufacturers by button makers. However, once the button makers switched to using synthetic substances themselves, it meant the ball manufacturers would have to cope with shinbones before they were cleaned up, and they were just too fastidious to deal with that.

Super Crystalate balls have been in use in snooker since 1973.

# — 4 —

DISCOUNT Tony Blair's tiresome prattle about "Cool Britannia." England, as I have always known it, endures. When I first arrived in 1950, railway station coffee was served in a chipped cup with a floating fatty milk skin. Given one inch of snow, an Arctic blizzard by tabloid standards, flights were canceled and trains were delayed for hours on end. *Plus ça change, plus c'est la même chose.* Hurrying to catch a 9:45 Virgin train to Birmingham on a cold, wet Wednesday, February 23, 2000, I arrived at Euston Station just in time to join a crowd accustomed to unsettling news. They were not to be disappointed. Suddenly the letters on the big board flipped to announce that my train, as well as many others, was to be indefinitely delayed. Fortunately I was able to catch the 9:15, already fifteen minutes late, seconds before it jolted to a start. There seemed to be no more seats available in coach class, so I opted for first, paying the premium.

"Would you care for an English breakfast?" the cheerful, red-coated stewardess asked.

"Yes."

"There will be no tea or coffee this morning."

"Why not?"

"Our boiler has broken down."

"Are we going to be very late?"

"That depends on how long it takes us to get past Watford. We're in a queue. There's been a power failure."

We arrived in Birmingham only twenty minutes late, and I took a taxi to the offices of *Snooker Scene,* in Cavalier House, in the suburb of Edgbaston. Clive Everton is the publisher and editor of *Snooker Scene,* the game's Talmud, for which he also writes monthly tractates. He has been publishing the journal, aided by a staff of four, since January 1971, when he invested in an initial run of 3,000 copies that sold out immediately. In the late 1980s, its halcyon days, *Snooker Scene* enjoyed a circulation just short of 22,000 copies, but it now sold no more than 9,000 copies, mostly to subscribers. Distribution is the problem. W. H. Smith's, the largest vendor of newspapers and magazines in the U.K., has culled smaller-circulation magazines from its shelves to make room for more videos and CDs. Even so, Everton said, "We turn a small annual profit providing we count our time worth nothing."

Since we first met, Everton has acquired *Pot Black,* a rival publication, boosting *Snooker Scene*'s circulation to 16,000. A big, immediately likable gray-haired man, sixty-two years old in 2000 and a father of five, Everton is as comfortable discussing the novels of Jane Austen as he is the snooker-table problems of Ronnie O'Sullivan, whom he adjudged "the most extraordinary natural talent the game has ever known," but a player who has yet to win the Embassy World Championship in the Crucible Theatre, in Sheffield. "Basically," said Everton, "it's only the Crucible that counts. Winning or losing there is what defines everybody."

Everton was British Junior Billiards champion for the under-sixteens and again and again for the under-nineteens and was a leading amateur even when he was making his way in journalism and broadcasting. In 1980, he rose to forty-eighth in the World Professional Billiards and Snooker Association (WPBSA) rankings. His career was blighted by a disk problem, surgery not much help, but he continued to write about "the theatre of cruelty" for the *Guardian* and the *Sunday Times*. On the opening day of the 1978 world championship, BBC's TV producer drifted into the pressroom and said to Everton: "Would you like to do some commentary for us this week?"

"Yes, when?"

"In about twenty minutes."

He proved to be the most articulate of commentators, and since then has been a fixture on BBC-TV snooker telecasts, along with John Virgo, David Vine, Willie Thorne, and Dennis Taylor, the latter a former Crucible champion.

Surprisingly, said Everton, given snooker's largely working-class following, it was the daily broadsheets (the *Telegraph, Times, Guardian,* and *Independent*) that provided the fullest coverage. "As far as the tabloids are concerned," he said, "it's football, football, and more football."

Inevitably, our luncheon chat turned to Stephen Hendry, who had failed to win a ranking title since he had last prevailed at the Crucible. In a worrying interview, going into the Masters Tournament at Wembley early in February, Hendry had said, "I've done more in my career than I could ever have dreamed about. Winning my record-breaking seventh title at Sheffield last May fulfilled my last remaining ambition. I'm on record as saying even if I didn't win another title I have achieved my goals. I am very happy with my life."

Everton, who rates Hendry the best player ever, said, "I hope you realize that snooker makes for an ascetic life. It means practice and doing drills at the club every morning. Day after day. Week after week. Most of the players haven't got as much time as they would like for girlfriends. Hendry is now a happily married father of a three-year-old boy. Some argue that it has disturbed his focus."

So in snooker, as in writing—as Cyril Connolly once observed—it would seem to be the perambulator in the hall that is the artist's worst enemy.

## − 5 −

MY BOOKS, accumulated over fifty years—many of them lugged to and fro across the Atlantic more than once as we shuttled between Canada and England—have lately become both a burden and a rebuke to me. Terry Kilmartin's translation of Proust still unread. Ditto *Moby-Dick* and *Ulysses* and Byron's poetry in one fat volume. But I have finally dug into my seven-volume edition of Gibbon's *History of the Decline and Fall of the Roman Empire*, acquired maybe twenty-five years ago. The acerbic wit and the soaring prose have made for joy unconfined. Again and again I have stopped to read choice passages to Florence:

"Twenty-two acknowledged concubines, and a library of sixty-two thousand volumes, attested to the variety of his inclinations; and from the productions which he left behind him, it appears that both the one and the other were designed for use rather than for ostentation."

I took volume two of *Decline and Fall* with me to Birmingham and, on the train ride back to London, I laid my homework aside—a stack of back issues of *Snooker Scene* provided by the helpful Clive Everton—and cracked it open, only to discover that the supremely intelligent and cultivated Gibbon took the Jews to be the most obnoxious and degenerate people:

"The sullen obstinacy with which they maintained their peculiar rites and unsocial manners seemed to mark them out a distinct species of men, who boldly professed, or who faintly disguised, their implacable hatred to the rest of human-kind." Furthermore, "Their peculiar distinctions of days, of meats, and a variety of trivial though burdensome observances, were so many objects of disgust and aversion for the other nations, to whose habits and prejudices they were diametrically opposite."

This, surprisingly, from a literary master who well understood the origins of bigotry. Taking into account the torture and murder of the Roman Empire's earliest Christians, for instance, he wrote, "If the empire had been afflicted by any recent calamity, by a plague, a famine, or an unsuccessful war: if the Tiber had, or if the Nile had not, risen beyond its banks; if the earth had shaken, or if the temperate order of the seasons had been interrupted, the superstitious Pagans were convinced that the crimes and the impiety of the Christians, who were spared by the excessive lenity of the government, had at length provoked the Divine Justice."

Gibbon was also aware that in the Middle Ages sex-starved monks, in their solitude, entertained themselves by inventing sufferings of their primitive martyrs:

"It is related that pious females, who were prepared to

despise death, were sometimes condemned to a more severe trial, and called upon to determine whether they set a higher value on their religion or their chastity. The youths to whose licentious embraces they were abandoned received a solemn exhortation from the judge to exert their most strenuous efforts to maintain the honour of Venus against the impious virgin who refused to burn incense on her altars. Their violence, however, was commonly disappointed; and the chaste spouses of Christ were saved from the dishonour of even an involuntary defeat."

In a footnote, Gibbon credits Jerome, in his legend of Paul the Hermit, with the bizarre story "of a young man who was chained naked on a bed of flowers, and assaulted by a beautiful and wanton courtesan. He quelled the rising temptation by biting off his tongue."

Dismissing these early attempts at pornography as "extravagant and indecent fictions," Gibbon swallows whole canards about the Jews. In Cyrene, he would have us believe, the Jews "massacred 220,000 Greeks; in Cyprus, 240,000; in Egypt, a very great multitude. Many of these unhappy victims were sawn asunder, according to a precedent to which David had given the sanction of his example. The victorious Jews devoured the flesh, licked up the blood, and twisted the entrails like a girdle round their bodies."

So much for my people's burdensome observance of the Mosaic code in relation to the consumption of meats. Gibbon can't have it both ways. Such gourmandizing by my brethren clearly put paid to the tradition of a strictly kosher cuisine.

## 6

BILLIARDS was the main event, snooker merely a sideshow, until along came the great Joe Davis (1901–78). He was the player, wrote Clive Everton, who took snooker by the scruff of the neck in the 1920s and 1930s and, by the sheer force of his skill and personality, hauled it into position as the premier billiard-table game:

> Without him, snooker would never have had a world professional championship. Without him, it would never have graduated from its early venues—a billiard hall in Birmingham, the back room of a pub in Nottingham—to Thurston's, the billiards holy of holies in Leicester Square, and from there to larger public venues such as the Horticultural Hall, Westminster.
>
> Without him, indeed, it would have been a different game; it was he who transformed it from a somewhat crude potting contest—"the sort of game you played in corduroys and clogs," as an old billiards artist Tom Reece acidly put it—into the present sophisticated

mixture of breakbuilding techniques and tactical complexities.

Variously dubbed "Mr. Snooker," "The Sultan of Snooker," and "The Emperor of Pot" over the years, Joe Davis, a miner's son, was born in a Derbyshire village. His venturesome dad later became a publican who also ran a football club, and welcomed apprentice boxers into his watering hole. Davis won his first amateur billiards championship in 1924, and went on from there to become all but unbeatable at the game. In dire need of dosh, he became a hustler, taking on miners in their clubs at pink pool. However, he proved so proficient at it that the miners obliged him to play left-handed. So the moxie Davis developed a skill that would later serve him well at the snooker table, enabling him to take on pots that would ordinarily have required him to use a rest, or bridge, a crutch that he disdained as unreliable. In 1924 the prescient Tom Davis wrote to the Billiards Association and Control Club (BA & CC) to recommend that it bless a professional snooker championship tournament. A. Stanley Thorn, the association's secretary, replied, "The suggestion will receive consideration at an early date but it seems doubtful whether snooker as a spectator game is sufficiently popular to warrant successful promotion of such a competition." Nevertheless, three years later an inaugural contest was organized, the el cheapo BA & CC creaming off half the entry fees to splurge on a trophy for the winner. The vigorish that Davis famously took home from a Birmingham billiard hall for emerging as the first world snooker champion in 1927 came to £6 10s; and insofar as Fleet Street was concerned, it was a nonevent in the same year that Jack Dempsey suffered the celebrated long count in Soldier Field in Chicago, thereby failing to regain his world heavyweight title from Gene Tunney. But when Davis took the Billiards Championship again in Thurston's in 1928, attention was paid.

Before it was flattened in the Blitz, Thurston's, wrote Donald Trelford in *Snookered,* was to snooker what Lord's is to cricket and Wimbledon to tennis. Or, he might have added, had his purview extended beyond his offshore island, what the old Montreal Forum once was to hockey:

> The match room was like a miniature House of Commons or the smoking room of a London Club, with leather seats and oak panelling. J. B. Priestley once said of it: "Beyond the voices of Leicester Square, there is peace. It is in Thurston's Billiard Hall, which I visited for the first time the other afternoon to see the final in the Professional Championship." (Joe Davis was beating Tom Newman, as he beat him in the U.K. final every year from 1934 to 39.)

Priestley concluded his paean:

> "When the world is wrong, hardly to be endured, I shall return to Thurston's Hall and there smoke a pipe among the connoisseurs of top and side. It is as near to the Isle of Innisfree as we can get within a hundred leagues of Leicester Square."

Following Joe Davis's 1928 triumph, just about everybody in his hometown of Chesterfield turned out to greet him, chanting his name, singing, his charabanc led by police and a brass band round the town square.

Davis's reign as world champion continued for twenty years, until his retirement in 1946, but there was hardly any money in it and he had to live off his wits, pleading for sponsorships. "I thought of every product," he said later, "that might conceivably—and sometimes inconceivably—have any bearing on billiards and snooker and then offered my services in endorsing them. I tried eye lotions and hair lotions, shirt makers and shoe makers, without eliciting the slightest flicker of interest. The only contract for endorsing a product that I obtained in those days was for Churchman's Top Score cigarettes, which I used to smoke."

During the Second World War, Davis earned his keep in show biz, stitching together a stage act in which his trick shots were magnified and reflected to the audience by a huge angled mirror. His book, *How I Play Snooker*, survives, still the definitive manual studied by young players.

Following Davis's retirement in 1946, snooker's popularity went into a sharp decline for a decade. In retrospect, in the opinion of Clive Everton, the game suffered from revolving too closely round one man: "By retiring from the championship (i.e., not risking his reputation), he devalued the game's premier event and, it followed, anyone who won it."

Snooker's second coming, indeed its immense popularity today (tournaments are broadcast in fourteen languages in

140 countries), can be attributed to television. And it all
came about by accident, as it were. What happened is that
in 1969 the BBC-2 TV channel, the first to convert to color,
required inexpensive programs in which color was an in-
trinsic component, and which was sufficiently seductive to
tempt viewers to rush out to buy the required sets. Snooker,
with its fifteen red and six colored balls on a green baize surface, obviously filled the bill, but some BBC-TV pundits
doubted its appeal. All the same, they took a chance on a
half-hour weekly show: "Pot Black." This proved such a surprising success that the Beeb went on to cover the highlights
of the championship tournament at the Crucible in 1976. A
year later they stepped up coverage to follow the top sixteen
players in that seventeen-day marathon, from initial rounds
right through to the finals, making for a hundred hours of
compelling TV; and the BBC also telecasts the Benson &
Hedges Masters Tournament at the Wembley Conference
Centre in London.

The Crucible Theatre World Championship final of 1985,
easily the most thrilling contest ever, is still the one everybody talks about—especially Dennis Taylor, snookerdom's
real-life Rocky. When I told friends in Canada that I was
going to be traveling on the tournament circuit, all they
wanted to know was, "Are you going to meet that guy with
the funny glasses?"

Taylor, a Catholic from Ulster, was born in Coalisland,
County Tyrone, in 1949. Going into the 1985 world championship contest, he was considered no more than an

affable also-ran. An also-ran of some distinction. After all, Taylor had qualified for two world semifinals as well as the 1979 final. He had joined the circuit in 1971, cueing for thirteen years before he won his first major title, the 1984 Rothman's Grand Prix. His luck changed in the 1983–84 season when he first adopted those outsize, upside-down eyeglasses that would become his signature and, according to Australian player Eddie Charlton, made him look like Mickey Mouse with a welding shield on. Those ostensibly comic but truly effective eyeglasses are worn so high on Taylor's face that he can look down the cue and through the optical center of the lenses, eliminating what had hitherto been a disconcerting distortion. The larger lenses also benefit him by providing improved peripheral vision.

Taylor took out Tony Knowles, who was ranked number three, in the championship semifinals—much to the consternation of the game's aficionados who now feared a mismatch of a final, with Taylor obliged to play against snooker's then dominant player and reigning champion, Steve Davis. Lamenting such a dim prospect, John Hennessey wrote in the *Daily Mail,* "What should be the most exciting climax to the sport's premier event is in danger of being reduced to a farce."

In order to be anointed world champion, a player must win eighteen frames in the final; if necessary, the contest will last through four sessions, running afternoons and evenings over two days.

Taylor's defeat in the final was a foregone conclusion and,

come the end of the first session, the seemingly outclassed Ulsterman was down a humiliating 8-0. Panicky bookies reduced the odds on a whitewash from 300-1 to 100-1 and, during the interval, the usually astute Clive Everton ventured, "Taylor looks three inches shorter. His head sunk into his neck. Even if he gets a chance now, he won't be able to take it. He's lost belief in himself—every shot will look horribly difficult to him."

Donald Trelford said to the *Observer*'s Hugh McIlvanney, "Another case of a nice guy coming second."

"He'll come third if he goes on like this," said McIlvanney, who went on to write, for an early edition of the Sunday *Observer*, a piece he had to drastically rewrite for later editions:

> Davis brings to his work the inviolable singleminded-ness that sets apart such champions as Nicklaus and Fangio, of whom it was said that he could drive through a crowd who were throwing beer bottles at his head without missing a gear change. What that single-mindedness inflicted on Taylor last night was painful to behold. Red-faced and seeming to sink even lower in his chair, looking more and more like a sick owl re-signed to being savaged by an eagle, he was humiliated beyond anything a nice man should be asked to suffer.

Hold the phone! Stop the presses! For Taylor rallied, fin-ishing the second session only 7-9 down, cheered on by the Irish fans in the audience. "The crowd," wrote Trelford, "go wild with applause for an impossibly brave comeback. Steve walks off stiffly, his face a mask."

The next session, on Sunday afternoon, concluded with Taylor down 13-11, and Clive Everton, still a doubter, confided to Trelford that Taylor would now be downcast—having played his best and still finding himself two frames down. There seemed to be something in that. For in the deciding evening session, Davis immediately went ahead 14-11, and soon enough 15-12. Then the recalcitrant Taylor, rallying yet again, leveled the action at 15-15. But it all seemed for naught when Davis, digging deep, edged ahead 17-15, now requiring only one of the three remaining frames to clinch the title. Never mind. Taylor took the next two, and the white-gloved referee racked up the balls for the final frame, as midnight approached.

Once all the reds had been potted, Davis was in front 57-44. He then potted the yellow (59-44) and fluked the green (62-44), which meant that Taylor had to sink all four remaining colors to win, while Davis needed only one. "It was the commencement of a ten-shot sequence," Everton later wrote, "which brought the championship to a climax and will forever be counted among the great moments in sport."

After some nervy seesaw play, Taylor finally took on and potted a risky brown, and then the blue and the pink. The score now stood at 62-59 in Davis's favor. The championship, and the £60,000 winner's purse, all rode on the last ball on the table. The black.

Taylor narrowly missed a double on the black, Davis also

failed, and when Taylor next took on a long pot that didn't drop, he thought he was done for.

Over to Trelford, who was lucky enough to be there:

> When he misses it Taylor clearly thinks he has lost. He goes straight back to his chair without daring to look at the table. Only when he gets there does he realize that the black is not a formality for Davis, requiring a very fine cut into the top pocket. Seven times out of ten, Davis says later, he would get it, but perhaps only three times out of ten under such pressure. The white is close to the cushion, so he has to play down on it, which tends to magnify the slightest error. The pocket he is aiming for is out of his direct vision. As he says later: "It's not difficult, but it's not easy." In the event he makes too thin a contact on the black, which rebounds a few inches away from the pocket, leaving Taylor a relatively straightforward shot for the championship.

Taylor potted the black and, in a TV sequence that is shown again every year during championship coverage, the exuberant Ulsterman is seen grasping his cue with both hands, raising it over his head in triumph, shaking hands with an incredulous Davis, and next looking into the crowd to point a finger at his wife, Trish, and his family.

A forgivably fulsome Everton wrote afterwards in *Snooker Scene* that it was a demonstration of all that was finest in the game, venturing that there was grace and sportsmanship not only from the highly popular new champion, but also from the deposed Steve Davis.

The *Irish Times* held its presses to carry the result. The people of Coalisland, where Taylor, a lorry driver's son, had been brought up in a house by the canal, sharing his bedroom with three brothers and four sisters, poured out into the streets in their pajamas and nightgowns to celebrate, parading round the town square. The BBC-2 telecast, watched by 18.5 million people until 12:23 a.m., set three records. It was the highest figure for televised sport in Britain, the largest BBC-2 audience, and the largest British television audience after midnight. To this day it ranks as the second-highest viewing figure, trailing only the ice-skating duo of Torville and Dean.

"Everybody still wants me to talk about the match," said Taylor years later, "and I still get a buzz every time I recall the final black. How can I get fed up with talking about a match that changed my entire life?"

The engaging Taylor, now fifty-one years old, recently retired from professional competition. He was still willing to chat about his astonishing triumph when I met him for late-night drinks in the depressingly utilitarian bar of the Novotel Hotel in Sheffield, after he had put in a long day as a BBC-2 commentator on the championship play at the Crucible. Blessed with a nifty line of comic patter, Taylor now earns his keep as an after-dinner speaker and exhibition player at corporate gatherings. Two of his stories, albeit embellished by repetition, are worth repeating here.

On a Canadian tour in 1974, he shared a Toronto hotel room with another player who was spellbound by the number of channels available on their television set. "Dennis," he said, "I'm going to buy one of these TVs and take it home."

On a tour of Northern Ireland with his friend Terry Grif-fiths, the 1979 Embassy World Champion, he appeared in Coalisland. Griffiths offered to demonstrate his "machine-gun" trick shot, in which the cue ball is made to glide slowly toward a pocket and a handful of reds are fired off rapidly to beat it there. "The only trouble is," said Griffiths, "I haven't got a machine gun."

A voice from the crowd quickly countered, "Don't you worry, Terry. We'll soon fix that for you."

Taylor readily agreed that Hendry was the best player he had ever seen, but he adjudged Steve Davis the superior tac-tician. "When I started out in the seventies," he said, "most of the top players were in their thirties or forties, but today they are in their twenties. And now Hendry is thirty-one. The competition is tough. Very tough."

## 7

JAMES THURBER once wrote that he lulled himself to sleep striking out the fat of the 1920s New York Yankees batting order. Murderers' Row. Babe Ruth, Lou Gehrig, Bob Meusel, Earle Combs, and Tony Lazzeri. I tend to drift off taking on Stephen Hendry at the Crucible, mercifully rescued by slumber before he demolishes me.

The estimable Phil Yates, snooker correspondent for the *Times*, agrees with Everton and Taylor that Hendry is unarguably the greatest snooker player of all time:

> If you . . . deal in hard facts and place trust in statistics there can be no other conclusion. Anyone who could argue against Hendry's claim could sell central heating systems in the Sahara . . . this is an ongoing tale of brilliance.
>
> Overwhelmingly, those who would question Hendry's right to be regarded as snooker's finest practitioner will, at some stage, use the name of Davis, either Steve or Joe. No one can deny they were giant

figures in the sport but there is a difference between the great and the greatest.

Hendry has earned that distinction, the right to be referred to, quite simply, as the best player ever to pick up a cue.

Even Steve Davis, a.k.a. the "Romford Robot," winner of seventy-three trophies and the man Hendry displaced as the game's dominant performer, has acknowledged his usurper's stature: "What Stephen has done is phenomenal. Great is an overused word in sport but it definitely applies to him."

I don't know at what age Ted Williams was first presented with a bat, or Tiger Woods with a golf club, but Hendry's parents, his dad then a greengrocer and now an Edinburgh publican, bought him his initial snooker table as a Christmas gift when he was twelve. "It cost them £137 from a shop in Dunfermline," he said, "and that present changed my life."

He was only thirteen when his mum and dad announced that they were separating. "This was the worst thing that happened to me," he said. "It was a tremendous shock because I never expected it. I just didn't have any idea they were not getting on. I was immersed in snooker and they had never had any fights or shouting matches. It was very sad for my little brother, and we went to live with my mum in a cramped council house." Hendry, who was distressed to have his mum struggling on her own, was later able to buy her a house "for the three of us to live in. Mum, me, and my brother. Then I bought one for my dad as well because I couldn't leave him out."

Hendry won the Scottish Amateur Championship in 1984, aged fifteen, the same year that he quit school, and in 1985 he signed a professional contract with Ian Doyle of Cuemasters. Doyle is his caring manager and surrogate father to this day. Hendry told me Doyle treated him like a potential champion from the beginning. "He saw to it that I didn't have to put up in dreary B & Bs for tournaments, but paid to book me into hotels where the best players on the circuit also stayed."

He was seventeen years old when he made his Crucible debut in 1986, and there is a touching photograph of him at that event in *The Embassy Book of World Snooker*: an impossibly slim, childlike Hendry, cue in hand, thoughtfully rubbing the back of his head as he ponders the spread of balls on the green baize. The veteran Willie Thorne, who had joined the circuit eleven years earlier and was now just short of being twice as old as Hendry, eliminated him 10-8 in the first round. Months later, the teenage Hendry reached the semifinals of the Mercantile Classic, only to be taken out 9-3 by Steve Davis. Next, the astute Ian Doyle put on his thinking cap and plunked £30,000 on the table to bankroll a learning experience for his young protégé, pitting him against Davis in a series of exhibition matches to be played in Scotland. Grand Master Davis promptly served notice that the youngster, albeit promising, was still an apprentice, winning all six of their exhibition matches. The very next day, a determined Hendry poked his head into Doyle's office. "I can beat him," he said. "I know how to beat him."

Hendry avenged himself against Willie Thorne in the Crucible's 1987 first round, beating him ten frames to seven, and he got as far as the semifinals before losing a squeaker 13-12. Then he sat down to watch Steve Davis win his fourth Crucible crown. However, in that same year Hendry served notice of snooker hallelujahs to come, emerging as the youngest winner ever of a ranking title, the Rothman's Grand Prix, and taking home a £60,000 prize.

In 1990 Hendry began to chisel his cartouche on the decade to come. En route to the Crucible, he won three world ranking titles and two major invitational events. Then he went on to defeat Jimmy "The Whirlwind" White 18-12 in the Crucible final, becoming the youngest world champion in the game's history.

The following year, Hendry, who has depended on the same cue since he was a thirteen-year-old, suffered a bad fright. When he was competing in the Rothman's Tournament in Reading, his cue was pilfered from a practice room in the Ramada Inn. Ian Doyle immediately offered a £10,000 reward for its return. Two days later, a man strolled into a local police station and claimed he had found the cue in a rubbish tip. Although the police were understandably suspicious, Doyle handed over a check for £10,000, no questions asked.

"Oh, my baby," exclaimed Hendry, kissing his cue.

"That £10,000 was a good investment," Doyle told me, "considering that Stephen went on to win another £5.5 million with that cue."

In the 1992 Crucible final, Hendry was trailing Jimmy White 14-8 but then took the next ten frames to win 18-14. A year later he victimized White yet again in the final, securing his second Crucible title.

In 1994, even as Steven Davis seemed to be enjoying a second coming of sorts, Hendry went into a tailspin, enduring one humiliation after another. In what threatened to become the season from hell, he lost three tournaments in succession to Alan McManus and two to Ronnie "The Rocket" O'Sullivan. He also suffered defeats in the first round by Fergal O'Brien and, oh ignominy, by Thai *amateur* Tai Pichet. The snooker press, sniffing blood, began to sharpen their pencils to scribble first-draft obits. The *Daily Mail*'s Alan Fraser pursued Hendry into the John Spencer Snooker Club, in Stirling, where he habitually put in seven hours of practice daily. "At twenty-five," he wrote, "Hendry's jowls are fleshier than previous vintage and a golf shirt commemorating the day Jack Nicklaus opened his Monarch Course at Gleneagles—where Hendry is a member—could not conceal the beginnings of a tummy." On balance, however, Fraser grudgingly concluded that reports of Hendry's demise might just be premature, his rivalry with Steve Davis newly intense, he noted.

"Steve is a superb player and nobody admires him more than me," Hendry told Fraser, "but nothing needles me more than him winning a tournament." And then, addressing his possible Crucible showdown with Davis, he went on to say, "I am probably more desperate to win this than any I have ever been. Basically, I want to shut everyone up. Everyone is talking a load of nonsense in the game. They say so-and-so is going to do this and so-and-so is going to do that. It's going to be the year of Davis, the year of O'Sullivan, the year of McManus, or whoever. Of course, people are entitled to blow their own trumpets. That's not what I'm on about. I know the way players do interviews. I recognize the digs they are having at me. I can tell when they're having a pop. Take Davis in Ireland when I lost to Fergal O'Brien after being beaten in Thailand. After winning the tournament, he said it was not the time of year to be having bad results. He was obviously having a go at me."

In Fraser's interview with the touchy Hendry, which was published on the morning of his first match at the Crucible, he noted that the Scot's shyness was often taken for arrogance. "As with Davis in his period of dominance," he wrote, "he wins too much (and too often) to be anything but an Aunt Sally for the hostile emotions of the audience."

Hendry countered, "They think I'm a miserable bloke more or less. I don't mind how many people hate me as long as I keep winning. To me, winning is everything." But he did acknowledge that Davis, also unpopular so long as he was dominant, began to attract lots of fan mail and big crowds once he became vulnerable, taken for a has-been. "I've probably got to get married," he said, "have a couple of kids, start losing and cry when I have lost maybe, before people start to like me."

In the event, there was no showdown between Hendry

and Davis at the Crucible in 1994, as Hendry met Jimmy White yet again in the final, and edged him 18-17 in what had to be a heartbreaker for the Whirlwind. Hendry managed that win even though he was coping with a fractured left elbow, injured when he slipped in his hotel bathroom ten days earlier.

Hendry won the Crucible World Championship title in 1995 and in 1996, and for his record-breaking seventh time in 1999.

When the players returned to the fray in the autumn, he not only won the British Open at Plymouth Pavilions for the third time, but also scored his sixth maximum break in competition in the final. Following his triumph—which was preceded by Hendry's season inaugural win of the Liverpool Victoria Champions Cup, worth £175,000—he pocketed a first-prize check for £62,000 plus a £5,000 highest-break bonus, which meant that he had earned a nifty £242,000 in the opening three weeks of the 1999–2000 campaign. However, his mood was still defensive. "When I was struggling last season," he said, "I got all kinds of things written about me and stupid comments. People high up in the WPBSA said I'd never win another title again, but I always knew I'd have the last laugh and I have done."

In November Hendry was eliminated 6-1 in the semifinals of the Regal Scottish Masters by his former practice partner, twenty-four-year-old John Higgins, who had already displaced him as number one in the world rankings. He lost another semifinal in Shanghai, in February 2000, this time to the still baby-faced, plump and pouting, twenty-six-year-old Stephen Lee. There was worse to come. In the next tournament, the Benson & Hedges Masters in the Wembley Conference Centre—which Hendry had already won six times—he went out 6-3 to Ken Doherty in the quarter-finals, even as he was being heckled by the crowd. Hendry's play had become erratic. Uncharacteristically, he had suddenly taken to jamming the jaws of the pockets on pots he would customarily have considered a given. Though hardly a whinger, wrote Phil Yates in the *Times*, "The evening's marvelous entertainment was tainted, however, by a small, unruly section of the crowd, who upset Hendry to such an extent that on leaving the auditorium, he lodged an official complaint with Jim Elkins, the tournament director, concerning their abusive behavior. It was not the first time Hendry had been angered by the spectators at Wembley."

Springing to Hendry's defense in *Snooker Scene*, Clive Everton noted that the Wembley crowd was "traditionally the most raucous in the game, and few will regard [Hendry's] complaint as sour grapes. Indeed, those journalists who follow the circuit week to week know that on many occasions, Hendry has kept quiet about illness, equipment problems and/or a substandard table for fear of being branded a sore loser. He is anything but."

## — 8 —

I FIRST CAUGHT UP with the snooker circuit at Wembley on the afternoon of February 12, a Saturday, taking in some of the quarter-final frames between Matthew Stevens and the ebullient John Parrott, who supplements his snooker prize money doing a shtick on a number of TV variety and game shows. At the time, Stevens was number six and Parrott number ten in the rankings. Parrott, a thirty-six-year-old Liverpudlian who had already won close to £3 million with his cue, had beaten that perennial loser, Jimmy White, in the 1991 Crucible final. Today he was not in vintage form. Neither was Stevens. Play was scrappy, slowed down by a seemingly endless exchange of safety shots, until Stevens won the first session of four frames, clearing the table in the last frame with a hardly exceptional break of sixty-two points.

Fans congregated in the unappealing restaurant rooms, stinking of stale cooking oil, where beer and fast food were available. Others trolled the corridors where various cuemakers had set out their expensive wares in makeshift stalls.

Souvenir videos showing Hendry, Ronnie O'Sullivan, Mark Williams, Jimmy White, Steve Davis, Cliff Thorburn, and other stars doing their stuff were also on sale, as were instruction books and posters. The far from ideal theater itself, which could seat 2,500, was less than two-thirds full, the Saturday afternoon audience largely middle-aged and working-class. I had never sat in one of these venues before and it was immediately obvious that visibility would be a problem. The two roving TV cameras following the play on the floor often obstructed my view, positioning themselves between the audience and the players lining up a shot. And the ridiculously small TV screen overhanging the table was no help.

"Ideally," Clive Everton told me, "a theater should take no more than 1,500 people, if they're going to see anything. Of course, the box office is marginal. The fans are required for the atmosphere. When you actually get to the Crucible, you will see that the reporters watch the play on TV in the press-room. They don't bother with the theater."

The halcyon days when snooker could attract an audience of 18.5 million viewers, as it did for the final round of the Davis–Taylor showdown, have long gone. The 2000 Wembley Masters reached 2.5 million viewers for the early rounds, the audience climbing to 5.3 million for the finals, still a highly respectable figure given how all TV audiences have declined since 1985.

To begin with, the hot-to-trot WPBSA offered TV coverage for a modest fee, but—sponsorship money aside—such coverage has long since become the association's largest source of income. But, as Everton pointed out over lunch in Birmingham, the WPBSA, in common with other sports associations, is now burdened with an enormous problem: the British government's ban on tobacco sponsorship, which is supposed to come into play in 2003. Happily, the Crucible World Championship Tournament has been granted an exemption until 2006, the year the Embassy contract runs out.

When I met Graham Fry, head of production for Trans World International, which produces both the Wembley and the Crucible tournaments for BBC-TV, he told me that the television contracts for both contests would be up for grabs in 2001, and that he anticipated a bidding war. Alas, should either ITV or Rupert Murdoch's sports-hungry Sky Network win the rights, snooker would go the way of Formula One racing, already nabbed from the BBC by the far richer ITV network: the flow of play would be interrupted by many an infuriating commercial break. As things stood, Fry said, snooker still attracted more TV viewers than cricket, and was second in appeal only to Wimbledon tennis and, of course, football. But the audience had diminished. "Some say snooker isn't as popular as it once was," he said, "because of the lack of real characters in the game today."

Such characters as were available, say Londoners Jimmy White and Ronnie O'Sullivan, two of the game's bad boys, were the biggest draws. "Our problem is," said Fry, "the average age of our audience is quite old. We are watched mostly by old-age pensioners. The WPBSA is determined to attract a younger audience, so there could be some changes in the works."

To this day, tournament elegance is the happy rule. Players wear bow ties, white shirts, dapper waistcoats, black trousers and shoes, and the referees are turned out in tuxedos and white cotton gloves. Now, unfortunately, there is increasing talk of outfitting the players in designer lounge suits to be provided by new sponsors, desperately sought after by snooker in common with other sports. Meanwhile, advertisements on the players' waistcoats are limited to the discreet display of logos over the breast pocket, usually promoting Highland Spring mineral water or Riley's, a manufacturer of cues and snooker tables. But Fry told me that the suggestion has been made that it would also be possible to stitch logos into players' shirt cuffs, which are often seen in TV close-ups as they stretch to line up a pot. Or, come to think of it, why not plaster the players in adverts from head to toe like F-1 drivers, those poor souls obliged to supplement their meager incomes by becoming human billboards? Among traditionalists, myself included, the fear is that a downhill plunge into vulgarity, in quest of profit and a "yoof" audience, is inevitable. It could end with the stately referees being supplanted by shapely young girls with bouncing blonde curls, wearing jiggly bras and micro-shorts.

# ~ 9 ~

I REJOINED the snooker circuit in Ireland in March.

In the summer of 1972 we rented a seaside cottage in Connemara, and one glance at the goods available in the food and clothing shops of Clifden and Roundstone was sufficient to establish that we were surrounded by poverty. The sixteen-year-old girl who traipsed barefoot across the potato fields to help out with the housework was, we discovered, illiterate. Her six brothers were all unemployed.

Happily, penury is no longer the rule in Ireland, which now seems to be one big fat Silicon Valley. "Are the Irish really richer, these days, than the British?" asked a recent issue of *The Economist*:

> [The Irish Economy] has been growing at breakneck speed—faster than any other country in the EU for each of the past three years. . . . Unemployment is under 5%. Labour is in short supply, even though people, reversing an old trend of history, are pouring

in from all over the EU, from Central Europe and
back from the United States to get jobs. Foreign
investors love the high level of Irish skills, especially
in computing. . . . Nearly a third of American investment in the EU is said to be going to Ireland, much of
it into high-tech companies. The "emerald tiger" is
veritably roaring.

The taxi driver who picked me up at the airport said the
value of his home had just about doubled in five years, and
then he asked where I was from.

"Canada," I said.

It was now all but impossible, he reported gleefully, to re-
cruit locals to do menial jobs in hotels and restaurants: "So
we recently flew over a thousand people from Newfoundland,
grateful for a chance to work at anything."

The Benson & Hedges Irish Masters in Kill, County
Kildare, is a party for the entire snooker tribe. Ostensibly
convivial, this non-ranking event is also a tune-up for the
unequaled pressure to come at the Crucible. Benson &
Hedges had set out complimentary packs of their cigarettes
on tables everywhere in the bar, only to have them swiftly
snatched up by the beat journalists in attendance. Courtesy
cars, laid on by our hosts, regularly spun us from the Citywest Hotel to Goffs, a ten-minute run. My first afternoon's
driver was troubled. One of his mates, he said, had suffered
a bad day. "His mum died of a heart attack at the foot of
the stairs this morning," he said, "and when his Da came out

of the first-floor bedroom, and saw what had happened, he also had a heart attack, tumbling down the stairs. They're both dead. Sean won't be able to watch Ronnie O'Sullivan tonight, and he was really looking forward to it."

Players bring their wives or girlfriends to this event, and often their mums and dads as well, and Benson & Hedges entertains everybody lavishly. Players, coaches, managers, beat journalists, and tour groupies all hunker down at the Citywest. Revels in the crowded, smoke-filled bar don't usually subside until five a.m., the players—except for Hendry, who is not to be seen there—luxuriating in the warmth of their admirers. The ebullient John Parrott, MBE, holding forth at what looks like a family table. Jimmy White traveling with an entourage I wouldn't like to run into on a dark night. An unshaven Ronnie O'Sullivan scribbling autographs for groupies who seem about to melt with pleasure.

Hendry is not a fan favorite. Scoring a century, he does not acknowledge the spectators' applause. Flubbing a simple pot, neither does he lean over the table, head hanging low, or bang his cue against the cushion, soliciting sympathy. Playing brilliantly or enduring a lapse, he remains imperturbable.

He puts me in mind of John Updike's memorable piece about the great Ted Williams's final game at Fenway Park in Boston. Life improving on art, Williams hit a homer in his very last appearance at the plate, but, circling the bases, head down, failed to tip his cap, and later declined to emerge from the dugout to recognize the wild cheers of the home-town fans. Immortality, Updike concluded, is not transferable: "The papers said that the other players, and even the umpires on the field, begged him to come out and acknowledge us in some way, but he refused. Gods do not answer letters."

"I don't smile much," said Hendry, when we eventually got together at the Gleneagles Hotel in Scotland. "Of course everybody wants to be liked, but I don't have to live with the fans." Then, actually smiling, he added, "If I'm not big with the blokes, the grannies adore me."

The Irish Masters is played at Goffs, actually a turf club, a venue for Irish bloodstock sales which first announced itself as an auctioneer in 1866:

> Mr. R. J. Goff respectfully informs Noblemen and Gentlemen that he will attend any Race Meetings, receiving due notice, to dispose of Winners of Selling Stakes, or conduct Sales of Bloodstock, and from his knowledge and experience of this branch of the business he trusts to give entire satisfaction and to merit continuance of the patronage he may receive.

Over the years Goffs has sold some seventeen Grand National winners, including L'Escargot and West Tip, and in 1985 it peddled Turkish Treasure for a then record 1.2 million guineas. The circular main building, with long rows of paddocks running alongside like barracks, squats on a 110-acre estate. Approaching it for the first time in a soft rain on a Thursday afternoon in March, the third day of play, I learned that, much to the chagrin of local aficionados, the two Irish contenders, 1997 world champion Ken Doherty and Fergal O'Brien, had already been eliminated. A prominent sign staked into the gravel announced SEAN GRAHAM BOOKMAKER IN ATTENDANCE. Punters were already queuing outside his office in one of the paddocks, the odds quoted on Hendry to win 3-1 and the odds on anybody scoring a maximum clearance of 147 quoted at 40-1. Hendry had already notched seven maximums, including the only two ever compiled in a final, the last of these in the 1997 Liverpool Victoria Charity Challenge. If Hendry or any other player were to manage the feat at the Crucible, he would qualify for a £147,000 special bonus prize.

Inside Goffs, vendors at makeshift stalls were already surrounded by customers testing cues for heft. Depending on which authority you credit, there are either six million or maybe three million snooker players in the U.K., the game being fancied by the very rich and the poor, skipping the middle class for the most part. So there are beautiful antique tables to be found in such London clubs as White's, Boodles, the Savile, and the Garrick, and beer-stained, serviceable ones in Labour and miners' clubs and the often sleazy venues where Alex "The Hurricane" Higgins (no relation to John), Jimmy "The Whirlwind" White, and many other pros served their apprenticeship, hustling or earning £100 a night for exhibition play.

Typical, perhaps, was the Canadian Cliff Thorburn, who in 1980 became the first non-British player to win the world championship. Thorburn learned his craft crisscrossing North America, hitchhiking, hustling local hotshots here, there, and everywhere. "I'd go into town in this old mechanic's uniform, which was absolutely filthy," he ventured in *Playing for Keeps*, his autobiography, published in 1987, written with the help of the ubiquitous Clive Everton.

> I'd stop by a gas station and stick some grease over my hands. I'd remember the name of the gas station so that I could say I worked there, and go into town to a pool room.
>
> In Odessa, Texas, once I beat a guy for about $700 and he says to me, "Where are you from, boy?"
>
> "Seattle, Washington."
>
> "You work round here?"
>
> "Yeah."
>
> "Where?"
>
> "At the Mobil station down the road."
>
> "Yeah, which one?"
>
> I said such and such on such and such a highway.
>
> He said, "No you don't."
>
> I said, "Yes I do."
>
> He said, "No you don't. I own the place."

It's worth backtracking here, to look in more detail at the 1997 final of the Liverpool Victoria Charity Challenge, which Hendry eventually wrapped up with a maximum. He appeared to have an early lock on the best-of-seventeen match, coasting to an 8-2 lead against Ronnie O'Sullivan, but he went on to drop six frames and, presto, the match was tied 8-8. "In the last frame," said Hendry, "I broke off and Ronnie played one of the best safety shots I've ever seen to put me in trouble. I managed to play a good safety shot myself, and then he left me with a long red. The white was under the balk cushion and the red was about a foot from the top pocket, three or four inches from the side cushion. As soon as I saw it, and saw there was a natural angle to hold for the black, I knew I would take it on. I also knew that if I missed, I would probably lose the frame there and then."

He didn't miss. Instead, he potted the long red, the black, and fourteen more reds and blacks, followed by all the colored balls; he later pronounced that final the highest-standard match he had ever played.

But in 1998 the then thirty-year-old Hendry was adjudged not only deficient in charisma, but also a performer in decline. He had won only one tournament in 1997, perhaps the worst of his defeats being administered by his erstwhile Crucible patsy, Jimmy White. The Whirlwind bid him bye-bye 10-4 in Sheffield's opening round. In an obit that turned out to be a tad premature, Alasdair Reid suggested in the *Sunday Times* that Hendry's new-found frailty revealed him as more sympathetic than he had appeared in his years of "metronomic mastery of the baize."

Hendry responded, "People think I'm miserable and cold, but I'm really a very passionate person. I'm very good at hiding my feelings so I come over as cool but inside it's a different story and I'm nervous like everybody else. It's important not to show that to your opponent."

After eight years as *numero uno* in the world rankings, Hendry had slipped to number two. However, he gallantly refused to endorse the popular explanation for his loss of edge—his recent marriage to Mandy and the birth of the young couple's first child. Possibly, he suggested, he was merely suffering from green baize fatigue. "While my mates were mucking about and having a good time," he said, "I'd be at the snooker club. For the past thirteen years I've been practicing snooker five hours a day, six days a week."

"One minute," Steve Davis once said, "you're the greatest thing since sliced bread, the next you're just bread and everyone's taking a slice."

Noting that Davis was now ranked number fourteen, Hendry said, "I've seen the trend, Steve Davis being the obvious example. But it's hard to say whether the process is inevitable, because there have only been me and Steve in this position over the past twenty years. It's something I'd like to think I could avoid, but the situation is there and maybe the only way now is down."

He told a reporter that his dilemma was now similar to that of Davis. "When Steve stopped winning and I started to beat him, I would say things like 'He's not as strong as he was.' I haven't won for a year now, so I've got to expect them to say I'm finished. They don't say it to your face, it's always behind the scenes, a bit snide. You've just got to ignore it and show greater determination." And then he acknowledged his one unfulfilled ambition, a record-breaking seventh win at the Crucible, which is exactly what he managed in April 1999.

"I never lost faith in Stephen," said Mandy afterwards. "I knew that he'd come back."

She had met Stephen at a holiday camp in Prestatyn in Wales when they were both fifteen-year-olds. When he turned pro a year later, Ian Doyle banned her from accompanying him to tournaments, fearful of the distraction. He told his protégé that he would have to choose between snooker and Mandy, so Hendry gave her up. "Of course I was devastated," he said, "but I had to sacrifice one part of my life to make a success of the other. Mandy resented me tremendously and hated Ian for making me do it. She didn't speak to him for a long time. She still brings it up now and again, but there's no bitterness left. Maybe it's one of the reasons Mandy hates snooker. After all, I gave her up for the game, not for another woman."

But in 1994, ten years after they first met, Hendry and Mandy were married. She accompanied him to the Irish Masters, and I often came across her chatting with the other snooker wives or girlfriends, in the bar provided for the privileged at Goffs. Twittering pretty bleached blondes seated all in a row. Birds on a wire. Difficult to tell apart.

Goffs can seat 950, but once you factor in standing room, available on the main floor as well as in the first-floor balcony circle, it can cope with 2,500 fans. The Thursday afternoon quarter-final, John Parrott vs. Mark Williams, was thinly attended, most of the audience made up of the middle-aged and the elderly, or what my daughter Emma calls cottontops.

Unlike chess, which proffers an infinite variety of opening

gambits, the first man up in a snooker game always attempts the same shot. In *How I Play Snooker,* maître Joe Davis wrote:

> The opening stroke, as described when this book was first published, caused a little trouble here and there because I described it as usually played by professionals and it has been shown by correspondence that the weaker grade players are not accurate enough to play the outside ball of the second row. They can quite safely play the outside ball of the top row, using the same method and achieving the same safety position, though with a different split of the pyramid, and that is what I now advise for all except the well above average. For the latter I would advise them to take careful note of the ways in which a properly placed and packed pyramid will open after various contacts with the top outside red, and with a contact with the outside red of the second row.

Ideally, glancing the cue ball off the outside red in the first or second row of the pyramid, an opening player brings it back tight against the balk cushion, leaving nothing on for his opponent. If he is really lucky, he will ease the cue ball back to a dead stop immediately behind the yellow, snookering his opponent for a how-do-you-do. On occasion, this can lead to a seemingly endless exchange of safety shots, until one player errs or suffers an unfortunate contact, making a pot available to his opponent.

John Parrott beat Mark Williams, the provisional number one in the rankings, 6-3, and then the two of them took their places at a counter on the main floor to autograph programs for the fans. Waiting outside Goffs in a downpour, no courtesy cars available, I soon got a lift back to the hotel from a Dublin couple, a retired army officer and his wife. "These are boom times for us," said the officer's wife.

"The great-grandchildren of people who fled the potato famine," said the officer, "are now returning from New York and Boston, looking for opportunities in computer chips."

Even so, there were problems.

"Years ago," said the officer's wife, "if you saw a black man on the street in Dublin, you knew he was a medical student, but nowadays. . . . Well, things change everywhere, don't they?"

Going into the Irish Masters, Hendry, a three-time winner of the crown, had already taken seventy-one ranking titles and compiled 497 centuries. The player who came closest to that mark, the now forty-one-year-old Steve Davis, had scored only 275, although he had played eight years longer.

In an evening session, a quarter-final, Hendry disposed of Alan McManus 6-2 but was adjudged "efficient rather than outstanding" by the *Snooker Scene* Sanhedrin. According to my notes, he played well enough to win, if only just, never extending himself. Fan favorite Ronnie O'Sullivan beat Matthew Stevens 6-4 in his quarter-final, but was fulminating because his picture wasn't hanging in Goffs with the other champions'. O'Sullivan had been stripped of his 1998 title after he flunked a drug test. "I won here before," he complained to reporters. "I hope to win it again. I mean, smoking a joint isn't going to enhance my performance. I know I still won it. But rules are rules. Maybe I'll bring a Polaroid and stick it on the wall."

After a late night in the Citywest bar, I wakened hung over on Friday morning, and flicked on the radio in my room for a weather report: "We are expecting rain in the south today and showers in the north. Thunderstorms are predicted for the west and easterners can look forward to another wet day."

Back at Goffs, it turned out that old pro John Parrott, who had competed in the Irish Masters every year since 1989 but had yet to win the tournament, also had a grievance. The disrespectful bookies had posted him at 66-1 to win the world championship. "It hurt me," he said. "It was an insult." Hendry took him out 6-1 in the semifinal, but was deprived of a potential maximum in the fourth frame. He had potted eight reds with eight blacks. Alas, in potting his ninth red he inadvertently fluked another one, and that was that. Hendry had now won more than £6.5 million at the table. Prior to the Benson & Hedges Masters, he had already said that if he didn't win another title he would have achieved his goals.

Did this mean, I asked Ian Doyle when we met for drinks in the hotel bar, that Hendry had lost his appetite for the green baize?

I should have known better than to put such a dumb question to a player's manager. On the contrary, said Doyle,

Stephen's will to win was still great.

The astute sixty-year-old bookmaker's son, a dapper Scot with a neatly trimmed little silvery mustache, enjoys an enviable reputation for integrity in an occupation more noted for its predators. "In order to be launched on the circuit," Everton told me, "young players will sign anything."

Doyle's Cuemasters organization represents twenty players, among them Ken Doherty, Ronnie O'Sullivan, Mark Williams, and the obnoxious Stephen Lee. Doyle attempts to sign players when they are as young as fifteen, acquiring sponsors to support them as they work their passage through the ranks. Riley's, for instance, has sponsored Hendry ever since he was a sixteen-year-old looking more like an altar boy than a hard-nosed competitor. Today his annual retainer, depending on whom you talk to, is at least £50,000 but possibly even £100,000. He charges £5,000 to appear at a corporate dinner, but doubles his fee if the affluent jock-sniffers also oblige him to hang out on the golf course with them all afternoon.

Doyle, his eye on the main chance, has taken his Cuemasters into the Internet, backed by a £10 million investment from Warburg Pincus, a City finance house. Doyle will serve as chairman of The Sportsmasters Network Ltd. (TSN), which will proffer the daily scuttlebutt from the Embassy World Championship tournament beginning in 2001 on www.TSNsnooker.com. The Internet site, which will also boast a comprehensive snooker archive, will offer on-line gambling, interactive game play, merchandising, and, at times, live audio commentary.

Friday turned out to be another late night. Seated alone at a corner table in the crowded hotel bar, well into the single malts, insufferably loud rock music pounding my ears, I grudgingly realized that it was now my reportorial duty to intrude on John Parrott's table. Or Jimmy White's menacing entourage. Or into the circle where an obviously aggressive Ronnie O'Sullivan was holding forth. Introducing myself, explaining that I was on assignment from *The New Yorker*, opening with a question calculated to charm:

"Tell me, Mr. O'Sullivan, what's your take on the Grand Inquisitor in *The Brothers Karamazov*?"

To which O'Sullivan was bound to reply, "I do believe, my dear boy, what you have in mind is *Crime and Punishment*, which I have always considered Feodor's *chef d'oeuvre*."

I didn't budge from my table. I didn't want to risk talking to Jimmy White, for one. That afternoon, as White had led his convoy through the lobby, the helpful woman at the front desk had said to me, "Jimmy's not as boorish as he used to be."

"He's mellowed?"

"I wouldn't go that far."

What am I doing here at two a.m., I wondered, when I could be at home in bed with Florence? Why am I drinking and smoking too much in this clamorous bar, a sixty-nine-year-old scribbler, further past his prime than even the faltering Steve Davis? A so-called cultured man who has yet to read *Tom Jones* or *Vanity Fair*, with time running out?

I once read somewhere that Billy Graham said he first found God on a golf course. He did not specify on which hole it was that he discovered he had a calling, not that it matters. In fact, I mention this bizarre epiphany not to mock the evangelist, but in self-defense. For just as Billy Graham connected with his Maker on the links, so I first broke with my faith at the age of thirteen—not due to a precocious reading of Voltaire or Darwin, which would have done me credit, but by frequenting poolrooms, snooker my liberation.

I was raised in an ultra-Orthodox home where we didn't switch on the lights, answer the phone, or light the wood stove in the kitchen on the Sabbath. Why, in my paternal grandfather's home across the street—ten of his fourteen children were still rooted there in those days—an aunt estimated how much toilet paper would be required over the Sabbath, and tore and stacked the sheets on Friday afternoons, because ripping off perforated paper was considered work, which was forbidden after sundown. With hindsight, I must admit that some of our religious practices were not that far removed from voodoo. Several days before Yom Kippur, for instance, I had to rotate a live rooster over my head (quickly, ever fearful of being shat on) while reciting a blessing that transferred a year's sum of masturbations, shoplifting expeditions, farting into my older brother's pillow in the bedroom we shared, and lesser sins, to that unfortunate bird. My God, think of what People for the Ethical Treatment of Animals would have to say about such an outrage today. The mind boggles.

Anyway, one Friday evening shortly after my bar mitzvah, I tempted God's wrath, daring to slip into the Laurier poolroom to challenge a stranger to a game of snooker. The heavens failed to open. I was not struck by lightning. Becoming a Friday evening regular at the Laurier, I had joined an alternative Jewish culture of sorts, where guys only a few years older than me—guys who were going nowhere—guys who would never discover the cure for cancer and didn't give a shit—smoked and drank beer on the Sabbath, swore, gobbled nonkosher hot dogs, and dated shiksas with impunity. Obviously snooker was a hell of a lot more fun than Talmud classes with Mr. Yalofsky in a back room of the Young Israel Synagogue. I hid my phylacteries under a pile of shirts in my bottom dresser drawer, where I also hid copies of the *Police Gazette* and *Sunbathing,* and never put them on again. Instead, I resolved to improve my cue work. It may have taken me more than fifty years, but that's what propelled me from St. Urbain Street to my vigil in a hotel bar in Kill, County Kildare.

A beat reporter I had joined for drinks in the hospitality bar at Goffs earlier in the day wandered over. At noon he had said, "Everybody feels sorry for fucking Jimmy White. He owns property worth more than a million quid in London." A considerate man, he now asked me to join his chums at a big table, unaware that I was already smashed.

"You know," I said, "when I was a kid my grandmother and great-grandmother used to stand at either end of a long kitchen table in that house on de la Roche Street, flipping and stretching a blanket-sized sheet of dough until they decided it was thin enough. Then they would roll it into one-yard lengths and go chop chop chop with kitchen knives, making noodles for the Sabbath chicken soup. *Lokshen.* I used to adore watching them at it, and I can't help wondering what they would say if they could see me here now."

"We're at the table over there," he said, retreating.

There are times when my obsession with time-wasting sports irritates the hell out of me. After my restorative afternoon snooze every day in London, I habitually venture out to pick up an *International Herald Tribune* at a newsstand on Sloane Square, and then I stroll over to the Crescent, that most agreeable of little bar/restaurants on the Fulham Road. I order an espresso and the Macallan and settle into the *Trib*, turning first to the sports pages to ponder the baseball or hockey scores, depending on the season. Okay, these are enthusiasms I was infected with as an innocent child and adolescent, long before I began to suffer from gravitas. But why do I also have to check out the standings in the latest golf tournament?

When Northrop Frye discovered that my friend Robert Weaver golfed, he was appalled. "I had no idea you indulged in executive sports, Bob," he said.

I've never golfed. To this day I don't know the difference between a birdie and a bogey. And yet—and yet—for reasons that I can't fathom, I worry about Phil Mickelson and the Canadian Mike Weir. I was truly pleased when another Canadian golfer, Ms. Lori Kane, finally won a tournament.

In Paris in the early fifties, drinking with other wannabe novelists at the Royal Saint-Germain or the Café Select, we seldom talked about our work or the books we were reading, discounting all that as sissy stuff. Instead, we exchanged views on Duke Snider's arm, Jersey Joe Walcott's real age, and whether or not Don Newcombe would ever win thirty games. Yes, we had all read and admired Jean Genet, but in spite of that we were real guys, you betcha.

I phone Florence immediately after breakfast.

"You sound like you must have smoked twenty cigars last night."

"Only three. Honestly."

Hendry met John Higgins in the Sunday Irish Masters final, quickly dropping the first couple of frames but taking the next two, scoring two centuries, bringing his total to 499. He lost the next frame and, soon enough into the second session, found himself trailing 6-3. The deeper young Higgins's concentration, the more frenetic was the dance of his eyebrows. He was clearly the fans' favorite, urged on, every time he came to the table, with shouts of "Come on, John!"

Sitting it out as the confident Higgins delivered one frame-winning clearance after another, a disconsolate Hendry looked like a schoolboy waiting outside the headmaster's office, where he was sure to be reprimanded. Taking his rare turns at the table, he seemed to be doing no more than going through the motions. Anticipating defeat. Determined to get over the embarrassment as quickly as possible. It would be presumptuous of me to suggest that I knew what Hendry was thinking, but he had the appearance of a man who wanted it confirmed that he could no longer do it—which would liberate him from the tyranny of daily practice and the tensions of the circuit. Free at last.

"To beat Stephen 9-4, anywhere, any time," said Higgins in another one of those predictable, make-nice, post-match interviews, "you've got to play at your best. He wasn't at his best, but that's only because I kept him off the table for long periods."

If it was any consolation, Hendry's £23,550 runner's-up check boosted his season's tournament gravy to £394,350, top of the prize-money list.

Sunday night, Hendry made a surprising if fleeting good-sport appearance in the hotel bar, quaffing a beer, joshing with some of the other players and tournament regulars, and then slipping away. An exuberant John Higgins was also in attendance. Actually, it was in his semifinal against Jimmy White that he had really distinguished himself. HIGGINS WIZARDRY CONJURES A 147 ran the headline in the next day's *Irish Times*. "Occasionally," wrote John Watterson, "they live up to their nicknames. The 'Wizard of Wishaw' did last night. John Higgins stepped up to the table for only the third time in this year's Benson & Hedges Irish Masters at Goffs and breathlessly shattered the record books.

"In 10 minutes 26 seconds, the 24-year-old audaciously pocketed all the reds and the colours for the competition's first ever maximum at Goffs."

Higgins's perfect frame was a thing of beauty to behold and did something to illuminate (for me, in any event) the obsession with sports shared by most male North American writers of my generation: my old friend Wilfrid Sheed, for one, who once wrote, "Sports constitute a code, a language of emotions—and a tourist who skips the stadiums will not recoup his losses at Lincoln Center or Grant's Tomb."

Look at it this way: if Higgins could make a maximum, or David Cone pitch a perfect baseball game, then just maybe, against all odds, a flawless novel was possible. I can't speak for other writers, but I always start out pledged to a dream of perfection, a novel that will be free of clunky sentences or passages forced in the hothouse, but it's never the case. Each novel is a failure of sorts. No matter how many drafts I go through, there will always be compromises here and there, pages that will make me wince when I read them years later. But if Higgins could achieve perfection, maybe, next time out, I could too.

Maybe, maybe.

The truth is, I tend to identify more closely with the suddenly sore-armed pitcher—Dwight Gooden, once King of the Ks, now no longer capable of throwing heat. Or Cone, pitching his perfect game in 1999 and, as I write, standing at 3-11 for the 2000 season. Once a novel is finished, my conviction is that I've lost it and will never be able to write another one.

Two years after I published my last novel, *Barney's Version*, a reporter phoned from Toronto. "We're doing a survey," he said. "What are you working on now, Mr. Richler?"

"Hey, I'm sixty-eight years old. Every novelist writes one too many, and that's the one I'm working on now."

# — *10* —

AS USUAL, early one morning in August, I climbed upstairs to my studio in our dacha on the shores of Lake Memphremagog, tea tray in hand, and sat down at my long plank table, ready to begin work. I could no longer make out the cigarillo burns and tea stains on the table, because it was now buried end to end in snooker books by various hands, newspaper clippings, photocopies, computer printouts, and stacks of *Snooker Scene* and tournament programs and press releases. I had just had time to flick on the power on my electric typewriter when the phone rang. It was an old Laurier poolroom chum who was still driving a taxi at the age of seventy-three. Last time I had run into him—outside that singularly ugly warehouse where the Canadiens now play hockey of a sort, the Molson Centre—he had been trying to flog tickets for that evening's game. "So," he said, "you became a writer and I became a scalper, and we're both *alter kockers* now." We exchanged phone numbers. I promised to meet him for lunch one day, but I had never called. Now he was on the phone at seven-fifteen a.m.

"Have you seen this morning's *Gazette?*" he asked.

"Not yet."

"Maxie Berger died."

"How old was he?" I asked, because this information is of increasing interest to me.

"Eighty-three. I want you to write something nice about him. He was a good fighter. A *mensch*, too."

"I'll call you soon, Abe, and we'll have that lunch."

"Yeah, sure."

H. L. Mencken once wrote, "I hate all sports as rabidly as a person who likes sports hates common sense."

George Bernard Shaw was also disdainful:

"It is a noteworthy fact that kicking and beating have played so considerable a part in the habits of which necessity has imposed on mankind in past ages that the only way of preventing civilized men from kicking and beating their wives is to organize games in which they can kick and beat balls."

Or each other.

Back in the days when I used to hang out in poolrooms, boxers were greatly admired by my bunch, some of whom could rattle off the names of the top ten in each division, as listed in Nat Fleischer's *Ring Magazine*. I had hoped to qualify for the Golden Gloves, but had been taken out in a qualifying three-rounder; my ambition then was not a Booker Prize or a perch on the *New York Times* bestseller list, but a Friday night main bout in Madison Square Garden, sponsored on radio by Gillette razor blades ("Look sharp! Feel sharp! Be sharp!").

At the time, I believed snooker to be a game played only

by working-class hooligans like us. I was unaware that Montreal's most elite men's clubs (the Mount Royal, the Mount Stephen) boasted oak-paneled rooms with antique tables. All right, that was naive of me. But I thought then, and still think, that no sport is without its class or racial baggage.

Where I come from, hockey and baseball appealed to every class and faith, and our distinctions were limited to where we could afford to sit. Since then, however, we have suffered the National Hockey League's ostensibly mindless expansion into the American sunbelt, a move actually informed by a subtext seldom mentioned. The owners hope eventually to acquire fan support by offering rednecks the only team sport left that is just about 100 percent white.

In the thirties and forties we counted football, golf, and tennis as strictly WASP as sliced white bread. We associated football with universities fastidious enough to have Jewish quotas, and golf and tennis with country clubs and resorts that wouldn't tolerate any Jews whatsoever. A down-and-dirty sport like boxing, on the other hand, belonged to tough kids out of Italian, black, Polish, Irish, and Jewish mean streets. Jack Solomons, one of ours, was the promoter with heft in London, and Joe "Yussel the Muscle" Jacobs called the shots in New York, where the great and near-great trained in Lou Stillman's gym. And welterweight champ Barney Ross, the son of a Talmudic scholar, gave us bragging rights.

In those days, boxing-beat hacks in Toronto had not yet been muzzled by political correctness. Describing a 1934 fight, one of them wrote: "For once, the Gentile barracking brigade will have to choose between the lesser of 'two evils,' when Sammy Luftspring and Dave Yack, a pair of Hebes, battle for supremacy at Frank Tenute's Elm Grove show at the Mutual Street Arena on Monday night." Not much later Lou Marsh, of the *Toronto Daily Star,* got to cover what was, as he put it, "an honest-to-Henry grudge fight between a Celt and a son of Moses," Sammy Luftspring versus Chick Mc-Carthy. The good news was this promising "slugfest" had attracted an attendance of 6,000—a record for Canada—"of which 5,795 talked turkey to the box office staff." Luftspring won a unanimous decision, but not before, wrote Marsh, "McCarthy opened the final round with a right-hander that made the aggressive little Jew boy lean like the Tower of Pisa."

A couple of days after Maxie Berger died, both the Toronto *Globe and Mail* and the *National Post* ran obituaries, noting that Maxie had briefly been world junior welterweight champion. Lacking the earlier verve of the *Star,* the tame *National Post* headline ran:

BOXER WAS LOVED

IN THE BRONX,

A STAR IN QUEBEC

Fought Five World Champions

He dressed well

and was popular

with women

In common with other newspapers, the *National Post* featured a silly photograph of Maxie, obviously retrieved from an ancient Canadian Press file. It harked back to the days when newspaper photographers in a hurry could be counted on to honor their own code of clichés. Photographing a novelist, they had him hold his latest book to his chest. Snapping two politicians shaking hands, they enjoined them not to look at each other but to smile menacingly sincerely into the camera. Dispatched to shoot a photograph of a real estate developer who was launching a hospital building campaign with a $25,000 donation, they got the donor and recipient to pose together clutching a four-foot-long replica of the check. I used to drink with one of those photographers when I was a teenager writing for the now long-defunct Montreal *Herald*, filing for two cents a line. Late one afternoon he told me that he had been paid fifty bucks by Nat Sugarman, who was running for alderman again in our district, to attend his debate with Herb Feingold, who also coveted a job that came with advance real estate information that could be worth plenty. "Now listen to me," said Sugarman, "you don't load that fucking camera with film because I'm not paying for that. But every time I hold up my pencil like this—watch me, see, I'm now holding up my pencil—every time I do that, you leap out of your chair to go flash flash flash. But whatever that shit Feingold says, you never take his picture. Got it? Good."

The incongruous photograph of Maxie showed him assuming his ring stance, leading with his left. But he is standing in the corner of a room, wearing an open-necked sports shirt and trousers belted high, addressing a blank wall. His swept-back hair suggests that it was brilliantined or that he had just got out of a shower.

"Clean up good, Maxie, for Christ's sake. You know how long it is since they took your picture for the papers?"

Cauliflower ears. Soft, dim eyes. Scarred eyebrows. Pulpy nose. Swollen knuckles. And no wonder. Over the wasting years the New York mob had fed Maxie to Fritzie Zivic, Beau Jack, and the great Sugar Ray Robinson, among others. Maxie took on Sugar Ray in Madison Square Garden in 1942, and was knocked to the canvas twice before the referee stopped the fight. Maxie wanted to continue but the referee shouted at him, "Do you want to get killed?"

The son of immigrants out of a Polish *shtetl,* Maxie had an education limited to elementary school, after which he went to work as a grocery delivery boy. He learned to box at the YMHA, on Mount Royal, which was then in the heart of the city's working-class Jewish quarter. He won a silver medal in the British Empire Games in the 1930s before turning pro, fighting out of the Bronx. Married four times, on his retirement he returned to Montreal and opened a custom-made shirt business where the smart guys could acquire those ghastly white-on-white shirts, inevitably worn with initialed cuff links and what we used to call one-button-roll sports jackets, with outsize padded shoulders.

I first encountered Maxie in the forties in the Laurentians, our minor-league Catskills, at the Castle des Monts Hotel in Ste. Agathe. A seething Maxie came roaring out of the hotel pursued by a hollering wife. When we shot *The Apprenticeship of Duddy Kravitz* in 1974, I made sure there was a small part for Maxie. The *National Post* obituary writer noted that Maxie was "like a character in a Studs Terkel novel," but Terkel never wrote a novel. The obviously nice man who had written Maxie's obit also had it that "he became a stockbroker in the early 1960s, profiting from the 1960s stock market boom." Actually, he served as a factotum for a brokerage house. In those days he would occasionally turn up in the Montreal Press Club, then in the Mount Royal Hotel, and I would chat with him there, an uncommonly gentle man who had taken too many punches to the head in close to a hundred fights. He was out of it for the last ten years of his life, a sufferer from dementia.

R.I.P., Maxie.

# ⁓ *11* ⁓

ON FRIDAY EVENING, April 28, waiting for Cliff Thorburn
to arrive, I sat alone at a table in the bar of the grim Novotel
Hotel in Sheffield, only a block from the championship action
in the Crucible, which I could watch on the TV set in the corner. We had a nine o'clock appointment, but Thorburn had
still failed to show by nine-thirty. I didn't really mind, because
the barroom traffic was not without interest. I was acknowledged with a wave, more in the nature of a dismissal than an
invitation, by two giggly groupies in miniskirts whom I had
first encountered at the Irish Masters. They settled like bait
into stools at the bar, displaying themselves to advantage. And
soon enough they hooked two guys in black leather jackets,
one of them sporting a Dallas Cowboys T-shirt.

When the groupies teetered off on spike heels to confer in
the ladies' room—arguing, I imagined, as to whether to com-
mit or wait on events—their two gleeful suitors exchanged
high-fives, and the more fastidious one amazed me by dipping hastily into a pocket for a tube and spraying his open

mouth. Then the girls were back. The men ordered a round and began to caress their backs with authority, establishing territorial rights.

Ten-fifteen and still no Thorburn. The evening's play at the Crucible over, the bar was now overcrowded and many couples were standing about, their drinks at risk of being jostled in the crush, ready to pounce should a chair become suddenly available. Again and again I had to turn away increasingly skeptical drinkers who were after the empty seat at my table, assuring them that I was waiting for a guest.

We were into the tournament's final weekend, so the suits had begun to arrive from London, among them the doctor who did the urine tests and dour Peter Middleton, chief executive of WPBSA, who paced up and down barking into his cellular phone. The suits were monitored by a patrol of formidable wives, not so much dressed as upholstered. Hair swept high, secured in back by a tortoiseshell comb. Jackets with padded shoulders, worn unbuttoned. Brooches adorning front-porch cashmered bosoms. Pearl necklaces. Big skirts and sensible shoes. Every time one of them crossed from the bar to mount the five steps to where the tables were set out on a platform, the planks rocked in rhythm with her heavy gait. These middle-aged women put me in mind of those stalwart Tory MPs' wives common to the decent John Major's era, Home County Boadiceas who posed arm in arm with their abashed husbands in the gardens of their weekend cottages in Kent or the Cotswolds, assuring the swarm of Fleet Street predators, even as they cautioned them not to trample the herbaceous borders, that they would stand by James or Roger or Geoffrey, who had been caught slinking out of a massage parlor, or humping a bimbo who had since sold her tale of woe to *News of the World,* or accepting a *pourboire* from al Fayed for favors rendered, or sharing a bedroom with a fetching young man in an auberge in Dieppe—only because it was cheaper than renting separate bedrooms, and anybody who suggested otherwise would hear from the solicitors.

I gave up at eleven p.m., retreating to my tiny bedroom, much the worse for too many single malts. The next morning Thorburn phoned to apologize. He had been a guest at a banquet and had forgotten our appointment. "It's not like me," he said. "I never do that."

"I'll catch up with you in Toronto this summer," I said.

Back in the sixties when Thorburn was still just another poolroom hustler, constantly on the road, crisscrossing the continent, he dipped down as far as San Francisco at least once, working a joint called Cochrane's, earning some $2,200 on one bonanza day. "I was getting better all the time and I was starting to get some backers," he wrote in *Playing for Keeps.*

There was one guy, whose name was Roy Bell. He was a mulatto. He always wore a hat and always carried a gun. I was so naive I thought that being with a guy who had a gun was quite safe.

He said to me one day I was going to play Skinner the bus driver across the bridge in Oakland. We parked the car and to get into this place we had to walk along a corridor which was about fifty feet long. It looked a little nasty in there. There was one light bulb for the whole place apart from the lights over the table. This Roy made the game and I was so much better than Skinner that I was soon up $600 or $700. Then I noticed a chap watching me who was a friend of Skinner's. He had a gold chain. The chain was off his neck and he was swinging it. He said: "There ain't no white boy ever gotten out of this place with Skinner's money."

But my backer had a gun so I just kept playing. I was so dumb. I won one more game and I looked over and the fellow was smiling at me. He pulled his jacket aside so I could see a gun in a holster. I thought: "He's got a gun. Roy's got a gun. That's one all."

Roy came over and said: "Cliff, I'm sorry to have to say this but I think you're going to have to lose back all the money we've won."

I said: "No way."

He said: "Look, you've got to do that. Plus, to be on the safe side, you should dump some of our money."

So I just stopped trying, not making it too obvious. We got out in one piece but it could have been fairly serious if Roy or myself had started to mouth off at them. It was good that Roy knew the score. Without him I'd have been in a lot of trouble.

Born in Nanaimo, British Columbia, in 1948, Thorburn was abandoned by his mother and spent two years in an orphanage before he was claimed by his father and grandmother, who brought him up. A far from model student in Victoria, he claims he made it into grade ten only because his ninth-grade teacher said, "I passed you because I don't want to see your goddamn face any more."

At sixteen he quit school, tried out unsuccessfully for the Kansas City Royals, and emerged as a poolroom hustler, winning five dollars here, dropping ten dollars elsewhere. Pilfering seventy dollars from his grandmother's purse, he tried his luck in Vancouver, and moved on from there to Yorktown, Saskatchewan, where the Salvation Army offered him a bed. Next he hopped a freight heading for Toronto, but he must have snoozed through that stop because he ended up in Montreal. Montreal, where the players to beat were Leo Levitt (whose 147 clearance was commemorated by a plaque in the Windsor) and "Atomic" Eddy Agha.

Continuing on the road, Thorburn worked as a dishwasher. He slept in friendly slammers. He put in time on a garbage truck. Winning some, losing some, he got to play against guys named Suitcase Sam, Oil Can Harry, and the Whale, his game constantly improving. It was risky, and hard work, too; Thorburn once put in fifty-four nonstop hours in San Francisco to win a thousand dollars, at thirty bucks a game, from a player known as Canadian Dick. Ahead of him, however, lay fame and riches on an offshore island. In his prime year he would earn £200,000 at the table, and tool around in a £45,000 Mercedes.

Undisputed Canadian champion from 1974 through 1978, he began to commute to England in '73, six months after his first marriage had broken up, and that's where he first encountered the man who would become his nemesis: Alex Higgins, snooker's original bad boy. "Higgins was in London at the time," he wrote, "and somehow he asked me if I wanted to play snooker for a fiver a game. He said he'd give me a 40 start. Being the gentleman I am, I only took 28. I don't think he won a game. All I remember is Higgins at the top of some stairs, I'm running down the stairs, I still haven't been paid, and he's got a ball in his hand, threatening to throw it at me."

Four years later Thorburn qualified for the Embassy World Championship Tournament, which was being played at the Crucible for the first time. He knocked out Dennis Taylor 18-16 in a semifinal, but was taken out 25-21 in the final by John Spencer. Pocketing his runner-up purse, he flew home and bought a car, the first he had ever owned, and began to work the exhibition circuit, such as it was. Racking up 2,800 miles, he played twenty-three shows in twenty-two days. He was back at the Crucible in 1978 and 1979, only to be eliminated in the first round on both occasions. But in 1980 he beat Alex Higgins 18-16 in the final to become world champion, as well as being rated number one by the WPBSA. "For Cliff Thorburn," wrote Clive Everton, "the world title was a poisoned chalice. He did not receive the recognition as world champion that he had expected, or indeed that Terry Griffiths had received the previous year. He was and is well liked in Britain, but because much of his art is that which conceals art, because his outstanding virtues are unfashionably those of steadiness, consistency and determination, the British public did not take to him as they tend to take to players more flamboyantly skilled or more adroitly presented to the media by their managements."

As he was so notoriously slow at the table, Thorburn was dubbed "The Grinder" by Alex Higgins. Others—taking his natural elegance into account, as well as that jaunty hairbrush mustache—pronounced him the "Rhett Butler of the green baize."

Following his championship win, Thorburn repaired to Toronto to compete in the Canadian Open, which was to be held at the Canadian National Exhibition (CNE) in August. No more than a sideshow in a fun fair, complained Everton.

At the time, it was estimated that some 200,000 people, not all of them on welfare, played snooker every day in Canada's 2,500 poolrooms, 150 of which could be found in and around Toronto. Thorburn's capture of the world title made little impact on Canada because, as Everton justifiably noted in *Snooker Scene*, neither the Canadian media nor the Canadian public regarded snooker as a bona fide sport along with golf or tennis. Snooker, he ventured, was socially suspect, stuck with a disreputable image. And the play conditions at the CNE were a travesty, largely due to the ineptitude of CBC-TV's lighting engineers: "Dazzling highlights were reflecting from the tops of the balls and there were deep shadows behind and, it appeared, almost everywhere. If the referee stood too close this too threw a shadow."

The fastidious Everton was understandably appalled by the informality that ruled at the CNE finals:

A temperature in the 80s meant that Thorburn and Terry Griffiths, usually among the game's most immaculate dressers, felt obliged to discard their ties as marbles of sweat dropped from brow to table. The dress standards of the crowd were, understandably, casual in the extreme. But since the screen in the home does not convey heat, the pictures either created or reinforced the impression that snooker is played by young men in open-neck shirts and watched by both sexes in jeans and tee-shirts. One memorable figure opposite the black spot was resplendent in peaked baseball cap, black beard, overalls and singlet. We must remember to send him a ticket for the final night of the Benson & Hedges Masters.

In any event, Thorburn won his third successive Canadian Open and the winner's purse worth $9,000, and returned to England, moving into his new house in Walton-on-Thames.

Alex Higgins, Thorburn's truculent foe, eliminated him 5-4 in an early session of the 1983 Irish Masters, and only a week later they got into a fight in a bar after Thorburn happened to sit next to the girl who was with Higgins. "Thorburn, you're a Canadian cunt," said Higgins, "and you can't fucking play either."

Thorburn floored Higgins with a punch to the jaw, and then people came between them, holding both men back.

"Let's all be friends," said one of them.

"Actually he says it two or three times," wrote Thorburn in his autobiography. "So, eventually, as we go to shake hands, I kick him right in the nuts."

The Canadian contingent, made up of Thorburn, Kirk Stevens, and big Bill Werbeniuk, won the World Team Cup at Reading in 1982, beating the England team, led by Steve Davis. Afterwards, Werbeniuk told reporters, "What I'm really hoping is that the BBC will sell the tape of us winning to the Canadian networks back home, because snooker needs it there. Even when Cliff won the world championship in 1980, the media interest didn't amount to much and didn't last very long. Snooker in Canada still has the image of guys playing each other for money in some pool hall."

Then, in 1983, Thorburn enjoyed another moment of glory in world championship play, scoring the first 147 ever recorded at the Crucible. Alas, he went down 18-6 to Steve Davis in the final, but as Everton wrote, "Although it was Steve Davis who departed the Crucible with his second world title, in every other sense it was Cliff Thorburn's championship, as the Canadian made the first 147 in the event's history. . . ."

Five years later Higgins and Thorburn clashed again, at the Scottish Masters, in a dispute over whether or not Higgins had hit a blue ball. Thorburn came from behind to win that match 9-8, and afterwards a seething Higgins caught up with him in the sponsors' room. "You're lucky," he said.

"Why's that?"

"You know, the bags of white powder."

Bingo. Those custodians of public morals, the squeaky clean gentlemen of the tabloid press, teetotalers one and all, overheard the exchange and it made sports-page headlines the morning after. Thorburn became the first snooker player to be punished for drug-taking, fined £10,000, and banned from two tournaments by the WPBSA. "It didn't stop there," he said. "My house was daubed with abuse and I actually got two death threats. People forget that I was world number one, but they sure remember the scandal. It was a one-off," he said, just possibly with his fingers crossed behind his back, "and I'll regret it for the rest of my life."

Moving back to McIntosh-apple Canada in 1986, he eventually slid to seventy-sixth in the rankings.

Pffft. Gone was the £45,000 Mercedes, and in 1993, Thorburn had to scramble to earn a piffling £10,000 on the circuit. "I lived like a millionaire for a while," he said. "The best bits were getting to play golf with Arnie Palmer and Nick Faldo."

In 1994, at the age of forty-six, Thorburn was reduced to playing a teenager in a gray-carpeted cubicle in a concrete hall in Blackpool, in one of those qualifying rounds for the Crucible. "I find it disheartening," he told a reporter, "that after playing Jimmy White, for instance, in front of 2,900 people in the final of my last Benson & Hedges in '86, I come to Blackpool in January and there's the referee, my opponent, and myself. There are now 730-odd professionals and 680 of them are half my age. I played one kid last year who was only eighteen. I didn't know whether to shake his hand or pat him on the head."

The next year turned out to be a bummer. Thorburn failed in the qualifying matches for all the nine tournaments he entered, dropping to a humiliating ninety-one in the ratings. So in the spring of '96 he announced that he would not be competing on the circuit come autumn. "I'm not formally retiring," he said, "and if things alter over the next couple of seasons I might consider playing again."

Channel-surfing one summer evening in our cottage in the Eastern Townships, only a couple of weeks before I would finally get together with Thorburn in Toronto, I caught a snooker trick-shot exhibition on a sports channel. Willie Thorne attempted to enliven his performance with a tired line of patter and Thorburn, next man up, earned only sporadic laughter with his equally banal repertoire of knee-slappers. The contest was tiresome, even embarrassing. The truth is, most champions past their prime are strangers to dignity. I once saw Jack Dempsey referee a wrestling match in the Montreal Forum, threatening Gorgeous George with a theatrical fist for fighting dirty, the wrestler obligingly falling to his knees, pleading for mercy. Plangent Joe Louis lived long enough to serve as a greeter in a Piccadilly nightclub. Maurice "The Rocket" Richard used to do Grecian Formula hair-color commercials on TV. Where is Joe DiMaggio now that we need him, Paul Simon asked in that famous song, and when he finally met DiMaggio, the baffled ballplayer responded, "I

haven't disappeared. I'm doing Mr. Coffee commercials."
Multimillionaire Wayne Gretzky, still a young man, will do
TV promos for just about any product that will have him,
except, so far, Tampax. So clap hands for Ted Williams
and Sandy Koufax and Jean Béliveau, who have never been
seen peddling.

Joining me for lunch in Toronto, Thorburn came in from
his home in the suburbs, arriving right on time. We repaired
to Harbour Sixty, a first-rate steakhouse where I was allowed
to smoke cigarillos, a rare Ontario privilege.

"Care to start with a drink?" I asked.

"Only, you know, if you are, you know."

So we drank.

Fifty years old now, Thorburn was still a handsome man,
his eyes bruised, his manner tentative. Married for twenty
years, he had two sons; the eldest, nineteen-year-old Jaime,
was a student at Ottawa U., which made the self-conscious
street kid who quit school at sixteen justifiably proud.

"Would you care for wine with our lunch?" I asked.

"Only, you know, you know, if you are."

"Red okay?"

"If you are."

"But why did you move back here?" I asked. "You're much
better known in England than you are in Canada."

"I'd rather, you know, be a big fish in a small pond."

"What do you do now?"

"Well, there are maybe, you know, four or five tournaments
a year here. But it's tough to benefit from stuff off the table. I

do exhibitions." He also hoped, he said, to soon open a snooker club in the suburbs with a partner. "They're supposed to be starting a circuit in England for senior players, you know, in the autumn. Willie Thorne, you know, Ray Reardon, Steve Davis. I want to see him qualify. I'm planning to return for that, you know."

"What was it like for you in England when you were world number one?"

"I felt as welcome, you know, as a Russian hockey player is over here. Hendry is the best player I ever saw."

"Was the drug bust hard to take?"

"I had made a bad mistake, but it was only that one time. I was ashamed for my children, you know."

Thorburn struck me as likable but sad. A mournful man. Reticent. Our luncheon conversation proceeded by fits and starts. So, much as I admired the teenage hustler who had gone from playing the likes of Oil Can Harry and Suitcase Sam to becoming the first non-British player to take the Crucible title, I was relieved when the coffee came.

"Care for a cognac?" I asked.

"Only, you know, if you are."

I was. We did. Outside, before we got into separate taxis, I put a final question to him. "Tell me, Cliff, why did you become a professional in the first place?"

"I ran out of customers."

# ⟿ *12* ⟿

IT WAS ALL DUE to an incident involving another Canadian player, Kirk Stevens—who became famously addicted to snorting the ambrosia many a young Chelsea stockbroker favors with impunity—that the image-conscious old maids of the WPBSA introduced drug testing in the first place.

Stevens, born and bred in the Toronto suburb of Scarborough, was seven years old when his parents split up, and he was dumped from his school for truancy only six years later. He was still a teenager, but already competing on the U.K. circuit, when his mother perished in a house fire that turned out to have been ignited by an arsonist. He flew home, and when his girlfriend was threatened—"You're next," said an anonymous phone-caller—he hid in the bushes outside her house with a double-barreled shotgun in hand—for ten nights, a few weeks, or a couple of months, depending on which tabloid was paying him for his story. On the one hand, his mother's death left Stevens "beside myself with grief," but on the other, he told the *Sun* it inspired him: "Overnight I became a top-class player and I'd like to think that it had something to do with my mother. Maybe her tragic death gave me the willpower to succeed. I'll never know—but it was the making of me."

Thorburn had first met the teeny-bopper snooker prodigy in Canada in the summer of 1972: "People were queuing up to play me for a dollar or two a game. All of a sudden this young kid comes along. He was twelve and so short for his age that he almost had a side-arm type of action."

He asked to play Thorburn for two bucks, refusing a starting gift of seventy points, insisting on playing him level. He lost two games and forked over four dollars. "I'd never seen money like it in my life," wrote Thorburn. "It was like it had been in his pocket for six years and his pants had been washed about fifty times. I said to him that he probably needed the money more than me but he said: 'No, here you are. You earned it.'"

The next time they met was in the Canadian Championship Tournament, then open to amateurs as well as pros, and Thorburn beat him 6-1. However, the following year a twenty-year-old Stevens served notice that he was a big boy now, eliminating Thorburn 7-5 in a semifinal.

In the depraved seventies, according to Thorburn, poolrooms had become conducive to reefer madness (like, come to think of it, just about any of today's Montreal or Toronto schoolyards or shopping malls). Anybody who spent much time in the poolrooms of North America, he wrote, couldn't have avoided coming into contact with drugs or drug users:

"A lot of young guys sample stuff just for the hell of it then decide it's bad for them and just don't get involved any more. Somehow, Kirk got hooked."

Precociously hooked on soft drugs at the age of twelve, Stevens graduated to "the lady of my life. The coke. The White Lady" when he was nineteen. In a 1985 sizzling front-page *Daily Star* interview, I'M A DRUG ADDICT, he revealed that he once blew $30,000 on his habit in three weeks.

A thoughtful guy for all that, he told the *Daily Star* in that world exclusive that he wasn't telling his story to damage the image of snooker, or to attack his peers; he had "found the guts to tell the truth in the hope that it will serve as a warning to others—and young people in particular—of what cocaine can do to their lives.

"This is my story. Please read it. And beware."

Although he never actually won a WPBSA tournament, "cute, happy-go-lucky" Stevens was a boffo attraction on the circuit, what with his flash pop-star look, long, painstakingly coiffed hairdo, perfectly awful signature white suits, and entourage of groupies. Once rated as high as number four, he was better known by the snooker cognoscenti for usually playing "high as a kite." He managed these flights to nirvana without reproach until the 1985 Dulux British Open in Derby. In this tournament, a true shocker, it was revealed that many a snooker player fancied puffing ciggies more confidence-enhancing than anything on offer from sponsors Benson & Hedges or Embassy, and, good heavens, some were also given to clearing their nasal passages with powders not available in the neighborhood drugstore. I doubt that fans were astonished by the news, but the guardians of the WPBSA's honor were something else again.

Stevens beat Steve Davis 9-7 in the 1985 Dulux semifinal and then moved on to meet Silvino Francisco, a South African, in the final. The touchy Francisco (who thirteen years later would serve time in the slammer, after attempting to zip through the Nothing to Declare channel in Dover with a supply of cannabis hidden under the driver's seat) protested unavailingly, on the first evening of the final, that his opponent was, um, using an illegal substance. During a break between frames the next afternoon, he followed Stevens into the loo, accused him of being high, and shook him up a little to ensure that his point had been made. Then he blabbed to a *Daily Star* reporter, saying Stevens had been "out of his mind on dope" during the Dulux final, and the hotshot reporter broke the story during Embassy World Championship play. Next the maladroit Francisco compounded his sin by appearing in a hastily called Sheffield press conference wherein he denied that he had ever said any such thing.

WPBSA suits, intent on damage limitation, did not confront Stevens but took disciplinary action against the snitch. Francisco was accused of bringing the game into disrepute by giving an unauthorized interview, by delaying play during the Dulux final, and by physical and mental abuse of Stevens. He was fined £6,000.

The tabloids continued to feast on Stevens. SNOOKER ACE BEATS DEATH ran a June 1986 headline. Stevens had been rushed to St. Stephen's Hospital in Fulham in a coma. His press agent, the ubiquitous Max Clifford, said: "Kirk's illness has nothing whatsoever to do with drugs . . . it was a blockage of the lungs which caused breathing problems."

Then, in February 1988, the *Daily Star* was on the case again: KIRK BACK IN DRUGS CLINIC. Stevens, making another attempt to kick his habit, had booked himself into a Toronto clinic for a month's retreat.

The following March, Stevens confided to the *Daily Express*, in an exclusive about his battle with drink and drugs, that he had started "A New Life," being now a regular at AA meetings. At the time, he was ranked thirty-seven and he was enduring a qualifying round at Preston for the coming world championship tournament. "No one thinks I can play any more," he said. "When they get me in a draw now, a nice little smile comes over their face."

In September the onetime "Ice Cream Kid, snooker's best-looking star," who had become known as "Cokehead Kirk," was flogging his familiar story yet again, this time to the *Daily Mirror:* MY MOTHER'S MURDER And How I Stalked Her Killer," with a new wrinkle added to the tale.

"'It was November 22, 1977,' he begins, 'the 14th anniversary of Jack Kennedy's assassination . . . (when) they told me my Mum had died. She was mur . . . mur . . . ,' he stumbles on the word, 'Murdered.'"

The *Mirror* ran a follow-up story the next day: "COCAINE: I BLEW £250,000. KIRK STEVENS on the *Drug-Filled Years That Nearly Killed Him and Destroyed His Career*, although not necessarily in that order." "It is now a few months since Kirk Stevens got serious about trying to quit cocaine," wrote Anton Antonowicz. "But his nose sniffs. He makes frequent trips to the toilet. He knows you watch every tell-tale sign."

In this story, which I assume was well paid for, an obliging Stevens, slipping into his Lourdes mode, delivered some new information about the time he lay in a coma in St. Stephen's Hospital. "I've never told anyone about this before," he said. "They'd probably have said I was hallucinating or something, but I had a vision.

"It was a bearded face, just a . . . how we're programmed to conceive the face of The Lord or whatever. I saw that image. It was just a brief thing.

"I don't remember profound words. But it was a comfort, a calmness I still had when I came out of the coma."

Soon enough Stevens was back in Canada, working in turn as a property surveyor, a used-car salesman, and a landscape gardener. One day he found himself sixty feet up a tree with a chainsaw in hand. "I hate heights," he said later, "and I don't much care for chainsaws, so I got to thinking that maybe snooker wasn't so bad after all."

In 1997 he entered the World Amateur Championship Tournament in Zimbabwe, qualifying by dint of his play in the atrium of a shopping mall in Saint John, New Brunswick, where he had regained the Canadian Amateur title he had last won in 1978. Unfortunately, he was defeated in an early round in Bulawayo.

To give him his due, Stevens was not a quitter. In 1998, at

the age of forty, he turned up for a six-week grind of Plymouth Pavilions qualifying matches for major tournaments. Martin Johnson of the *Daily Telegraph* was there:

"Stevens' first competitive shot in Britain for five years was a break-off which ended with the white disappearing into a corner pocket, although he did play reasonably well to take a 2-1 lead (against Ian Sargeant of Wales). Frame six, however, was more in keeping with the overall tenor of the game, in which both players made about forty visits to the table. It was like one of those Sunday lunchtime frames at the British Legion, with players digging into their pockets for another 50p for the lights."

Stevens went down 5-2 to Sargeant and retired to his cheap B & B, and the next morning the loquacious Canadian agreed to blab to reporters yet again about drugs and his mother's murder, provided they produced their checkbooks.

In its April 2000 issue, *Snooker Scene* reported that Stevens—who, lest we forget, had registered a 147 in the 1984 Benson & Hedges Masters—was attempting yet another comeback, this time in the American Tour. Playing in Montreal in a tournament organized by Cliff Thorburn that offered a total of $27,500 in prize money, he beat Kirk Clouthier 6-3 in the final, earning $8,000.

Surely the most colorful if not the most talented of the once formidable Canadian contingent was Bill Werbeniuk. Born in 1947 in Winnipeg, Manitoba, Werbeniuk joined the U.K. circuit at the age of twenty-six in 1973. In 1982–83, his vintage season, he was a member of the Canadian team that won the World Cup, and ranked as high as number eight. He reached the final of the Lada Classic, and got as far as the quarter-finals in the Crucible before being taken out 13-11 by Alex Higgins. From then on it was a downhill slide, with Werbeniuk calling it quits after he sank to number thirty-three in the rankings.

Conventionally described as gargantuan, Werbeniuk, who weighed 20 stone (280 pounds) in his prime, is still celebrated for a charming precedent he established with the U.K.'s Inland Revenue: for a time, it allowed him to claim his legendary intake of lager as tax-deductible. Justifiably so, for Werbeniuk suffered from a hereditary nervous disorder that made his cue arm tremble—a disability that could only be suppressed by a measured intake of lager, sometimes running to forty pints a day. A proven rate of consumption, incidentally, which renders risible William Hague's boast to have quaffed fourteen pints a day during his notorious spell as a teenage hooligan.

As a rule, on a morning when he was scheduled to compete in a tournament, Werbeniuk would wash down his breakfast toast and jam with eight pints of lager, and he would carry on to drink at least one steadying pint per frame.

For purely altruistic reasons, I deeply regret that the Inland Revenue has revoked Werbeniuk's right to indulge in tax-free booze, unarguably performance-enhancing in his case. Certainly not I but many a scribbler of my acquaintance could have profited from this precedent. The truth is that, for some of my literary peers, liquor is an essential lubricant of the creative juices, as necessary to them as, say, insulin is to the diabetic. Graham Greene once observed that there are writers born three drinks short of being able to cope with the world. Or, put another way, no booze, no muse.

Clive Everton told me that competing on the circuit is a hardship for non-British players. "They either fly in for a tournament, jet-lagged," he said, "or set far up from home and lonely."

Certainly that's the case with Alain Robidoux, the one remaining Canadian player on the circuit. Robidoux, who is managed by Ian Doyle, told Everton, "I get very homesick living in Britain. I couldn't go for more than a month without having to go home." In his case, to Quebec.

In April 2000, Robidoux, who had once stood as high as number eleven, had slid to fifty-first in the rankings. He had once soared as far as the world championship semifinals, losing 17-7 to Ken Doherty, but following that there came two years of misery that can be attributed to a disaster with a mythological subtext.

In 1998 the promising Robidoux sent his cue back to its elderly maker in Montreal for adjustments. Foolishly, it was dispatched in a case advertising Riley's. The affronted Montreal master craftsman smashed the cue, sending the pieces back to Robidoux. Rebuked, disowned, playing with an unsatisfactory replacement cue, a depressed Robidoux could no longer hack it on the circuit. After two years of ignominy he returned home to seek psychiatric help. His shrink advised him to rest from the game. "I decided to ignore snooker completely," he told *Snooker Scene*. "I have no idea who has won what tournament in the last six months and I don't particularly care."

# ~ *13* ~

I'M PLEASED to report that my countrymen, their subcultural origins notwithstanding, were far from being snookerdom's most delinquent sojourners. That office was first filled to the point of overflow by the game's original bad boy: the scrawny, far from self-effacing Alex Higgins, who once considered billing himself as "Alexander the Great" but ultimately had to settle for the sobriquet "The Hurricane." Over the wasting years, Higgins confirmed his hell-raiser's bona fides by wrecking hotel rooms, pissing in the nearest available plant pot, punching officials, tussling with opponents, heaving his cue at fans, head-butting a referee, scribbling apologies on toilet paper, indulging in reckless gambling, being bounced out of too many bars to count, and, for good measure, getting stabbed in the chest while living with a bimbo in a caravan. In his definitive *Embassy Book of World Snooker,* Maître Everton noted, "His projected tour of India lasted only one day, for he so offended the members of the Bombay Gymkhana Club by his drinking, the removal of his shirt and his insulting

behavior that the BA & CC of India, his hosts, put him on the
next plane home."

Higgins—nurtured on the mean streets of working-class
Protestant Belfast, the walls still graced by scrawled injunc-
tions to FUCK THE IRA—learned to handle his cue at an
early age in the Jam Pot billiard hall. A longtime fan of Lester
Piggott, and initially determined to make his name as a
jockey, he first crossed the sea at the age of sixteen to
apprentice at stables near Wantage. His career was aborted
because of his fistfights with the other stableboys. Higgins
turned pro in 1971, at the age of twenty-two, and won his first
of two Crucible titles only a year later. Reminiscing in 1999
about his accomplishments, he said, "I was a major force in
bringing snooker out of the shadows. I was the one that made
it a spectator sport, an entertainment. If I hadn't started the
ball rolling like that, I doubt that you'd have the young boys
in the game that there are now, because most of them were
inspired by Alex Higgins. I have created an audience of millions who have never even played the game."

There is certainly something in that, because for many
years the "People's Champion" was the game's biggest box-
office draw. I never saw him play, so I am obliged to rely on
the accounts of others. In her feisty *The Cruel Game: The
Inside Story of Snooker,* Jean Rafferty wrote: "It is as if at some
point during a match he moves from being Alex Higgins to
being The Hurricane. He's rolling, the crowds are with him.
But it's not the demonstration of power that his sobriquet
would suggest. If he resembles any natural phenomenon it

really isn't the hurricane sweeping everything before it by force. It's an electrical storm, incandescent, erratic, ripping the air apart in unpredictable bursts."

Such an astute observer of the game as Willie Thorne has said, "Technically, he is just a phenomenon. He does everything wrong: his stance is square, he lifts his head, his arm's bent, he snatches at some of his shots. Of all the pros, Alex would be about the last one you'd want to copy technically."

Fred Davis, on the other hand, has pronounced Higgins "the only true genius snooker ever had," an accolade which I fear Higgins would dismiss as an understatement.

Come 1981, Higgins was confined to a nursing home, "lying on his bed crying and swearing he would never look at another vodka," wrote Noreen Taylor in the *Mirror*: "From now on it was to be fruit juice only because he would shortly be teaching Steve Davis a few lessons on snooker.

"When the crying session ended, Alex reached under the bed and pulled out a bag filled with vodka miniatures and beer cans. The tears soon changed to giggles and the following night he was entertaining friends."

In 1996, Higgins, suffering from throat cancer, had a growth removed from his palate, and two years later he was diagnosed as cancer-ridden again. No longer of any fixed abode, scrambling, he was granted legal aid to pursue a High Court action against the WPBSA, claiming unfair treatment by their disciplinary tribunals.

Unable to track down Higgins, Anna Pukas, of the *Daily Express*, leaned on his chum Jimmy White for his phone number. White agreed to give it to her provided Higgins was handsomely paid for an interview. A sweetener of £10,000 was agreed to, but when Ms. Pukas phoned the former "People's Champion" he said, "I have no interest in talking to you or anyone else in the press. Why are you ringing me?"

After several botched attempts at a rendezvous—the emaciated Higgins now wary of being photographed—Ms. Pukas finally met up with him late one morning in Pearl City, a restaurant in Manchester's Chinatown. "Five minutes later," she wrote, "he had another of his mood swings. He was standing up, croaking loudly, his face so close to mine he was showering it with spittle. He didn't like newspapers."

Higgins flung the proffered contract away and fled. A day later he phoned to say that he would talk if the *Express* would also fork out for the tax bite on his £10,000 fee, but that a photograph would be "a grand in cash up front." They met in a pub, where Higgins insisted they immediately repair to the Allied Irish Bank round the corner for a perusal of the check. The bank manager confirmed that it was legitimate. "How long does it take to cash?" demanded Higgins. "Seven days? I haven't got seven minutes."

Ironically, it seems the impecunious Higgins never cashed his check, and the *Express* got its exclusive gratis. Ms. Pukas wrote: "Higgins has for years been dependent on the kindness of friends or fans who take him in. There can't be many of either left. He treats strangers like lackeys and friends like slaves. I never heard him say thank you to anyone."

Before 1998 was out, Higgins had endured forty-four

chemotherapy treatments for a cancerous lymph gland. When Brough Scott, of the *Sunday Telegraph,* sought him out in Belfast a year later, he discovered that Higgins was living in a pensioner's bungalow, looked after by his sister. Fifty-one years old now, he was back at eighty-four pounds, his weight when he had first crossed the Irish Sea at the age of sixteen to apprentice in a stable. "I started the industry of snooker," he said, "and I haven't got much thanks." And then he added, "I'm a wealthy man."

Following the removal of a lymph node from his neck, Higgins appeared in *Tobacco Wars*, a BBC-TV series. Gaunt, his tastebuds gone, he revealed that Peter McDonnell and Associates, a Dublin law firm acting on behalf of two hundred smokers in Ireland—The Hurricane among them—was suing Embassy and Benson & Hedges, two major snooker sponsors. Higgins accused them of offering players free cigarettes. Peter McDonnell argued that his client was entitled to £200,000 for the pain and suffering caused by what he claimed was a tobacco-related illness, and a further sum, unspecified, for lost years of earnings he could have counted on for the rest of his career.

In the year 2000, a *Daily Star* reporter espied Higgins in the Red Lion, Gatley, Cheshire, drifting from table to table, topping up his glass with leftover beer, as he couldn't afford to buy a pint himself.

A regular in the Gothic Bar and Grill, where Higgins was trying to borrow cash for a taxi, said, "Everyone round here has tried to help Alex at some point and you just get it thrown back in your face. We've all felt sorry for him, bought him beers, given him a few bob, even got him somewhere to get his head down. But he always ends up abusing your good deeds and we've all given up on him.

"He's a very sick man but he's still rubbing people the wrong way. His skill at the table has gone, his money's gone, and his friends all went a long time ago."

## — *14* —

HIGGINS'S HEIR—snookerdom's reigning bad boy, the erratic Ronnie O'Sullivan—is managed by Ian Doyle. "He is the greatest natural talent in the game," Doyle told me, and he went on to quote Hendry: "Stephen has said Ronnie has more natural talent in his fingertips than the rest of us have in our entire bodies."

In the 1997 world championship play at the Crucible, O'Sullivan, not dubbed "The Rocket" for nothing, earned £165,000 by potting a 147 in an incredible five minutes and twenty seconds in the very first round; and then, all too typically, dropped the next round 13-12 to Darren Morgan. Two years later he scored another maximum, actually his third, this time in the Grand Prix at Preston Guild Hall, but he was again retired in the second round.

Doyle, every client's surrogate dad, has arranged for the twenty-five-year-old O'Sullivan, who was rated number four going into the Crucible in 2000, to meet regularly with a "sports psychiatrist" treating him for depression. O'Sullivan is not only troubled, he is also defiant. Only recently he said, "You have Hendry on one table and you've got me on another and he has fifty people watching him and I have a thousand watching me. This tells me one thing—that I put bums on seats."

Indeed he does. Everton acknowledged in *Snooker Scene* that O'Sullivan is now a favorite of the fans, if not the gods. The chief magistrate added a stinging caveat: "Flawed virtuosity does often seem more attractive than sustained excellence."

O'Sullivan, capable of cueing with panache right-handed or left-handed, can be dazzling beyond compare, but he is easily frustrated, in which case his performance tends to disintegrate. "I can't pin down why I'm brilliant one day and another I'm not," he has said. "I wish I could. It's something in my head that's stopping me but I'm working on it, stressing the positive side."

In the 1997 Benson & Hedges Masters final, he led Steve Davis 8-4 and managed to lose 10-8. Brooding about the last session, he said it had probably been the worst two hours of his life: "My concentration went. I thought I'd won it. I'd got the highest-break prize and £155,000. I'd just played four of the best frames of my career, two centuries and a couple of nineties, and he hadn't potted a ball.

"I remember at the interval I thought he must be distraught in there, and I was buzzing. I only had to play two frames half as good and I was through. I could have gone 9-4 and I missed the yellow and after that I didn't see a ball until 8-8. In the last frame, I was cabbage. I couldn't believe what was going on. One minute you're going to win a massive tournament, the next you've lost it."

His biggest problem is his dad, to whom he is deeply attached. Ronnie O'Sullivan Sr. ("Ron's the name, porn's the game") used to run twenty shops in London dealing in porn books and videos. In 1991, when Ronnie Jr. was sixteen, his father was found guilty of stabbing chauffeur Bruce Bryan to death during a brawl in Stocks nightclub, on the Kings Road in Chelsea. The prosecution charged that Ronnie Sr. had been baiting, with racist taunts, a group who were out celebrating the birthday of Angela Mills, who just happened to be black and a former girlfriend of Charlie Kray, a notorious London gangster. He was sentenced to a lifetime in prison.

Ronnie Jr. believes his father was shafted. The cops had it in for him because he was a porn dealer. "And what's wrong with porn?" he has asked. "If it can keep just a few nonces off the street it can only be a good thing."

Complaining about the rigor of the sentence to snooker-beat writer Charlie Whebell, he said, "I couldn't believe it when he got put down for so long. OK, so he killed a man, but the geezer had smashed a champagne bottle over his head and, during the fight, my father had had two of his fingers almost sliced off. He stabbed the geezer in self-defence. Self-defence—and he gets life. It makes me angry when you read of those bloody nonces, those poxy paedophiles, killing little kids and then getting out after just nine years. And they call that bloody justice!"

Five years after Ronnie Sr. was incarcerated, his wife, Maria, who tended to the porn shop accounts in her own fashion, was sentenced to a year in prison for tax evasion, and the tabloids feasted on the compromising revelation that she had been born and bred in Sicily, just like Marlon Brando in *The Godfather*. Maria was sprung after seven months. But Ronnie Sr., currently held in Long Lartin, a maximum security prison in Worcestershire, isn't scheduled to be released until his adoring son is forty years old. O'Sullivan tries to talk to his dad once a day, and Ronnie Sr. often phones *Times* snooker maven Phil Yates in the pressroom when his son is competing in a tournament. "I'm the only geezer in here who reads the *Times*," he once said to him. "It's for the snooker reports."

The teenage O'Sullivan, a true snooker prodigy, became the youngest winner of a professional tournament and appeared unstoppable, going on to win seventy-four of seventy-six matches in qualifying rounds, before his father was imprisoned and his play became erratic.

And then his troubles escalated.

In 1996 the WPBSA fined him £20,000 and suspended him for two years, charging him with attacking a press officer during play at Sheffield, pissing inside the Plymouth Pavilions, and—oh dear, oh dear—lapsing into obscene language in a players' lounge. O'Sullivan, who has not led an unexamined life, responded, "I was a rebel. I was bitter. I had gone through a shitty time."

A year later his former girlfriend, eighteen-year-old Sally Magnus, who had once shared his nifty Chigwell mansion but who now earned £4 an hour as a print-shop worker, claimed O'Sullivan was the father of her baby daughter. *The News of the World* investigated:

> Scandal of Millionaire Snooker Ace Who Lives
> in a Mansion while his Daughter is on Breadline
> O'SULLIVAN HAS POCKETED £1,000,000 WINNERS'
> CHEQUES THIS YEAR WHILE HIS DAUGHTER
> SURVIVES ON HANDOUTS.

An outraged Matthew Acton reported, "Heartless snooker millionaire Ronnie O'Sullivan has fired his little daughter out of his life in the same clinical way he would pot a red.

"Straight into the corner pocket. Out of sight out of mind."

Heartbroken Sally revealed to the *NoW*, "I was a virgin when I met him, but we waited until I was sixteen before we did anything. He was a nice lover and a really nice bloke."

To begin with, O'Sullivan denied Sally had ever been his squeeze, so Sally took him to the Child Support Agency. He was forced to take a blood test that proved he was Taylor-Ann's dad, which he later acknowledged in a manner distinctly his own: "Do I ever see the baby? Nah."

"Ronnie is missing out," said Sally. "He might have all that money and cars and stuff but when I look at Taylor-Ann I know what is important."

*The News of the World*, its appetite for social justice insatiable, concluded its story with an appeal: "Do you know a meaner father than Ronnie? Contact us at 0171 782 3444 today or any day, 10 a.m. to 6 p.m. We'll ring you back."

Next, O'Sullivan was twice banned from driving either one of his BMWs, once for doing 130 on a motorway and another time for going 80 in a 30-mile speed-limit zone. According to another report, he had already crashed three BMWs. And there was worse news to come. GONE TO POT ran a huge headline in the *Express*: "Snooker superstar Ronnie O'Sullivan attacked an *Express* photographer yesterday after allegations that he had failed a preliminary drug test."

In 1998, that was, and the prissy executives of the WPBSA made him forfeit his Benson & Hedges prize money after he tested positive for marijuana.

Pot is most certainly not a performance-enhancing drug, but it is on the Sports Council's illegal-drug list. Other snooker victims of this statute have included not only such colonial stalwarts as Cliff Thorburn and Kirk Stevens, their alternative refresher of maple syrup unavailable so far from home, but also Paul Hunter, once fined £4,550 for marijuana use during a tournament, and Steve Ormerod, docked £800 when a routine tournament check of his urine revealed traces of cannabis. Assuming that these working-class lads, no different from their more privileged peers in Chelsea or Islington, indulged in cannabis between tournaments, why should they be deprived of this relaxant during the tense days of play?

With this in mind, and in the hope of providing them with an appropriate riposte next time they are confronted by the inquisitors of the WPBSA, I would like to pass on a story about Evelyn Waugh, gleaned from a friend's memoir.

During the Second World War, Waugh was appointed

aide-de-camp to a general, temporarily, as it turned out. One day the general summoned Waugh to his office. "Captain Waugh," he said, "it has been pointed out to me that you were drunk in the mess last night."

Waugh acknowledged that that was the case.

"Furthermore, I'm told you were drunk in the mess the night before."

Also true, Waugh allowed.

"This won't do, Captain Waugh."

Waugh replied, "Why should I change the habits of a lifetime to satisfy a passing whim of yours?"

"I ain't a good player," O'Sullivan has said. "I'm bloody fantastic."

ROCKET READY FOR LIFT-OFF AT THE CRUCIBLE proclaimed the *Guardian* on the eve of the year 2000 Embassy World Championship Tournament. En route to winning the last tournament prior to the championship showdown, the Regal Scottish Open, he compiled a 147 in six minutes and forty seconds, slo-mo by his standards, and trounced Mark Williams 9-1 in the final. His £62,000 prize catapulted him over £2 million in career earnings. In the press conference that followed his triumph, a jaunty O'Sullivan said, "It's the same wherever I am. The only player I've ever really worried about is me."

Whatever the outcome in Sheffield, the twenty-five-year-old Mark Williams would still be ranked number one. And Everton, who considered him to be possibly the best long potter in the game, accounted him a real threat at the Crucible. Other serious contenders were O'Sullivan, John Higgins, Matthew Stevens, and of course the reigning champion himself. HENDRY HUNGRY TO CLAIM EIGHTH CROWN declared Phil Yates in the eve-of-tournament *Times.*

Even as I packed my bag, bound for a morning train to Sheffield, charged with excitement, I was faxed bookmaker William Hill's odds on the players.

Stephen Hendry 3/1
John Higgins 10/3
Ronnie O'Sullivan 9/2
Matthew Stevens 9/2

Jimmy White, perennial loser in the finals, was listed at 66/1, and the once all but unbeatable Steve Davis was an insulting 100/1 shot.

## — *15* —

GIVEN THAT it is not brute force but natural talent, as well as acquired craftsmanship—both developed by putting in thousands of hours at the practice table—it is surprising that women players have not been able to compete successfully on the gents' WPBSA circuit, although a few have tried. They have been thrown a crust, a WPBSA circuit of their very own, but the prize money is piffling. In *Kissing the Pink*, a novel about snooker by Jane Holland, who competed on the women's circuit for six years, she complains about the vigorish available:

"If you win a tournament in the ladies' game, with the possible exception of the World Championships, you'll be lucky if you can afford a Strawberry Mivvi and the bus fare home.

"So why carry on? Not simply because we're suckers, though there is that. We play because we love the bloody game, with all its stomach-heaving ups and downs, its petty squabbles in the toilets, those moments of utter triumph when the last black trickles into the pocket and you know you've whipped [your opponent] like egg-white."

Zoë, the snooker-playing heroine of Ms. Holland's novel, is charged with scorn for the condescending male animals on the circuit, most of whom consider the women players freaks, and probably lesbian:

"Being a woman player is not a wise career option for the squeamish or easily offended. Let's face it, the vast majority of men who play snooker are those same men who hang half their bottoms over a work-site scaffolding and wolf-whistle mindlessly at anything in a skirt."

Problems for women players begin with their apprentice-ship years. Many of the working-class lads who have gone on to earn millions with their cues started out hustling in sleazy poolrooms or fine-tuning their skills in working men's clubs. There are 15,000 of these clubs in the U.K., 1,800 of which bar women from the games rooms. It was Henry Solly, a Unitar-ian minister opposed to "sodden drunkenness" among work-ing-class chaps, who set up the first of these clubs in 1862 to encourage "mutual helpfulness, rational recreation and social intercourse" among the unwashed; and these clubs barred women even as guests until the Second World War.

Today, while the Pontypool Working Men's Club still won't accept women members, it does welcome them for bingo three nights a week. Interviewed by Jane Czyzleska and Emma Lindsey of *The Independent on Sunday*, the bartender said, "They can be signed in as guests but can't have a membership card. This is where men come to escape from their wives."

Dipping a tentative toe into the sexual equality waters, the Earlsheaton Central Working Men's Club in Dewsbury, West

Yorkshire, includes 350 women among its 920 members, but the women are "house" rather than full members, and the snooker table is off-limits to them.

Such an unsatisfactory state of affairs has led to trouble for the Sunnybank Social Club in Silsden, near Skipton. A cluster of young women, obviously brazen, were discovered playing snooker and were promptly told to skedaddle. Happily, a couple of male gallants sprang to their defense. Mike Sutton, a retired electrical contractor, and Barnard Clarke, a fireman, threatened to take Sunnybank to court unless the club granted equal status to women. These shit-disturbers won the support of Robert Walter, the Tory MP for Dorset North, who promised to introduce a private member's bill into Parliament, which would amend the 1975 Sex Discrimination Act. "My bill will affect clubs right through the social spectrum," he has said, "from working men's clubs and golf clubs in the leafy suburbs to gentlemen's clubs in St. James." In other words, fat chance.

Meanwhile, the obdurate management of Sunnybank was unmoved even after the dominant woman player, three times Embassy Ladies' World Champion Kelly Fisher, on a guest visit, made short work of the club champion. Her plea that the club should allow women snooker-table rights was denied.

"We've worked on the assumption that men and women were classed differently," said Club secretary Rick Watson.

Even on the WPBSA circuit, the women continue to be patronized. The qualifying rounds for the year 2000 Embassy World Ladies' Championship were held in a club a couple of miles from the Crucible, and one of the contestants complained that the tables were virtually unplayable. "For a world championship I think we deserved better," she said. "The cushions on some of the tables were dead and the cloth just too slow. You couldn't get the balls to react properly."

Twenty-one-year-old Kelly Fisher won the title, her third, at the Crucible, worth the grand sum of £6,000, defeating nineteen-year-old Lisa Ingall 4-1 in the final. A couple of years earlier Ms. Fisher had become the first woman to win the championship at the Crucible—allowed access, in a rare act of noblesse oblige, to that most celebrated of venues on a free Sunday morning, when most of the fans could be counted on to be sleeping off hangovers.

In *Kissing the Pink*, Zoë, a thirty-year-old single mother of two, sets out to explain her obsession with the game:

> Everyone has a passion for something. For some women, it's a man. For rather more ambitious women, it may be a career. For a sad minority, it's crocheting or gardening or flower-arranging. I have a passion for snooker. It's not easy to explain why, but there's an air of romance about the game that I find irresistible. It's nothing glaringly obvious, just a subtle combination of things that keeps me enchanted: the weight of the cue balanced in my hand, the hum of the overhead light as it warms up, someone calling the score on a distant table, the tense smoky atmosphere of a league match, even the quiet click of balls

that comes back to me night after night in my sleep. But most importantly, it's a feeling of intimacy. The awareness that there's something happening between you and the table, something no one else can interfere with or destroy. Something an outsider could never understand. Every player experiences it differently, and that's what makes it special. It's a feeling of belonging in the midst of exile. Besides, the daily practice, the desire to play world-ranking tournaments, these represent my chance to get even with all those people who've tried to keep me out of snooker, and I refuse to go about it in a half-hearted way.

Elsewhere, Zoë muses:

The game responds to mood as the tide responds to the moon. With astonishing accuracy. I often wonder if this is the prime difference between male and female snooker players. Men are notoriously such insensitive bastards. Women are far more subject to mood swings; you argue with your best friend, your goldfish dies, you're having your period, the room's too hot, too cold, too noisy, someone laughs at your new outfit etc. It is those women players most capable of controlling their reactions to external stimuli who rise to the top of the game. It should come as no surprise then that some of those players become insensitised over time, almost masculine in their reactions. . . .

Jane Holland no longer competes on the circuit. Last heard from, she was reading English as a mature student at Oxford University. Her first book, *The Brief History of a Disreputable Woman*, a poetry collection, won her the £4,000 Eric Gregory Award for poets under thirty in 1996. Her intelligence is undoubted, but I wish she had written a nonfiction account of her years on the circuit rather than attempting a novel. *Kissing the Pink* is a potboiler, its soap opera plot predictable, redeemed only by those informed, deeply felt passages that deal directly with her snooker experiences.

# — *16* —

BETWEEN afternoon and evening championship sessions at the Crucible Theatre, I would repair to the bar of the neighboring Novotel Hotel, and there I would often espy the burly, self-important Peter Middleton, CEO of the WPBSA. Before we even got to sit down together, I reacted badly to his presence, familiar lines running through my head, uninvited:

> I do not love thee, Doctor Fell;
> The reason why, I cannot tell;
> But this I know, and know full well,
> I do not love thee, Doctor Fell.

Because WPBSA finances were in a mess, incompetence the rule, light fingers in the higher reaches suggested by some critics, on June 1, 1999, Peter Middleton had been appointed part-time CEO, his annual stipend £50,000. The then fifty-nine-year-old Middleton was already chairman of the Football League. Not your average grammar school boy, he had spent five years in a monastery before graduating from Hull University and joining the Foreign Office. After twenty-four years in the diplomatic service, he had gone on to accumulate an imposing c.v. as well as a reputation for truculence. In 1987 the Midland Bank had brought him in to oversee Thomas Cook, its travel business, which was not earning its keep, let alone turning a profit. He had gone on from there to Lloyd's, paid £250,000 a year to help sort out a legendary scandal. Backers known as "names," who had signed on with a Lloyd's syndicate—once considered the safest of institutions—bore personal financial liability if disaster struck. Strike it did, for five years running, and Lloyd's lost £11 billion. The names, many of them retired and not necessarily wealthy, lost their homes and had to empty their bank accounts to make good the damage. Banding together, they sued for kazillions, charging incompetence (or worse) on the part of certain syndicates, and eventually reaching a settlement of sorts.

Middleton had quit Lloyd's two years short of his contract's termination, following a disagreement with the chairman, and had signed up for a reported £1 million a year as European head of Salomon Brothers International. However, he had resigned in 1998 after he, um, "failed to establish his authority with some senior executives."

Joining me in the Novotel bar, this clearly capable but abrasive City man did not so much sit down as perch impatiently in his chair, obviously a chap with more important appointments to keep. Mind you, I have had trouble with men of consequence before. Once assigned by the *Sunday Times Magazine,* in London, to write a piece about Jewish life in the North, I phoned Sir Keith Joseph to ask for an interview. "I don't allow journalists into my home," he said.

"I understand," I replied. "I feel the same way about politicians."

Click.

I asked Middleton about his announcement that, subject to boardroom approval, traditional formal dress would be discarded for three 2001 tournaments (one each on BBC, Sky, and ITV) in favor of elegant casual clothes. This proposal had already earned a broadside from Professor Alan Thompson, of Edinburgh, who wrote to the *Telegraph* to protest snooker players being obliged to shuck their heritage only to be transmogrified into latter-day hippies:

"I was gravely disturbed by a recent statement on BBC TV that henceforth snooker players will be encouraged to 'dress down' and that there will be more informality in snooker tournaments. The essence of snooker lies in its quiet, dignified and courteous presentation (compared with some other sports). Formal dress—waistcoat and bow-tie—contributes to the image snooker players present."

Equally disturbed, I asked Middleton, why break with time-honored tradition?

"Do you ever see young people wearing such outfits themselves? They are alienated by the formal dress. They don't identify with it."

Had he inherited a mess at the WPBSA, I asked.

"Let's say things were badly managed for some time. I suffered open-mouthed disbelief at the incompetence. There will be a £1 million loss to the WPBSA this year through unsponsored tournaments. Disastrous contracts were signed."

Among them, I gathered, was the association's twenty-three-year-old contract with the Crucible. For only a day later Middleton rattled the snooker cage, announcing that the contract with the Crucible, due to expire in 2001, might not be renewed. Instead, the world championship might become a moveable feast, played in different venues each year. Dennis Taylor and Terry Griffiths, both association directors, thought there was a good deal to be said for this proposal, although Taylor weighed in with a caveat: "But I doubt whether any venue could create the same atmosphere as this place."

On the other hand, Willie Thorne and Stephen Hendry were opposed to such an unsettling innovation.

"It would be a retrograde step," Thorne told the *Times*. "When I used to live in Sheffield I'd get nervous just driving past the place, even in February."

Stephen Hendry said, "The world championship should always be at the Crucible. When you're a kid and you watch the game on television, that's where you dream about ending up. It's synonymous with what's good about the game."

"The Crucible is to snooker as Wembley is to football and Wimbledon to tennis," said Jimmy White.

Clive Everton interpreted Middleton's threat of road-show championship tournaments as no more than a negotiating ploy. As things stood, the Crucible, which could seat 980, and does not allow standing room, billed the WPBSA £125,000 for rental of the venue and, given its boarding house reach, it also claimed the bulk of the box office swag. So Everton considered Middleton's tactic justified. "However," he wrote in *Snooker Scene*, "the idea of changing venues every year is surely flawed.

"While this works for the Open Golf Championship, which attracts huge crowds, and Test Cricket, since one ground could not stage all matches in a series, Snooker is not in this category because gate money will only ever be marginal to its income."

Meanwhile Middleton did not endear himself to the gentlemen of the press, hitting them where their hearts were. He announced that in 2001, wherever the tournament was played, there would no longer be a free bar.

## ⌐ *17* ⌐

A LONG WAY from the Rachel Pool Hall of blessed memory, I approached snookerdom's holy of holies, the threatened Crucible Theatre, late on Saturday morning, April 15, in good time to catch the incomparable Stephen Hendry's opening match against the player—ranked number ninety-two—who was being fed to him; I anticipated that it would serve as no more than a useful warm-up exercise for the reigning champion. En route to Sheffield, the master breakbuilder had put another milestone behind him, notching his five-hundredth century. Striking a nice but unconvincing grace note, Hendry had already promised, "I certainly won't be taking Stuart lightly. There's no such thing as an easy draw these days."

His opponent, twenty-three-year-old Stuart Bingham—the 1996 World Amateur Champion, whom the bookies had posted at 300-1 to take the title—was equally gracious. Probably cursing his luck, he said, "I don't suppose anyone would pick Stephen Hendry out of the hat but playing him in my debut at the Crucible is a dream come true."

I made directly for the pressroom, or media center, where uniformed girls presided over a bar that offered tea, foul coffee, el cheapo wine, beer, and soft drinks. Middle-aged snooker mavens from the broadsheets (John Dee, Phil Yates, and of course Clive Everton) did not seem to mingle with the young hounds from the tabloids, ears perking up at the slightest hint of scandal. Drugs. Drink. Unacknowledged illegitimate progeny. Or a grabber of a first-person confession that could be gained by the promise of a fat check. FORMER WORLD CHAMPION BUYS HIS KNICKERS AT HARVEY NICHOLS: "I AM A CROSS-DRESSER." Or, even more devastating, CRUCIBLE SUPERSTAR SHOCKER: "I SUBSCRIBE TO THE TIMES LITERARY SUPPLEMENT AND NEVER MISS A PERFORMANCE OF THE MAGIC FLUTE, AN OPERA BY MOZART."

Some beat reporters operated from booths lining the walls, emblazoned with their own newspaper or press service logos, and others set up their laptops at long tables. None ventured into the theater, but would follow the action on the plentiful supply of TV monitors, many of them phoning in frenetic sixty-second state-of-the-play accounts to their newspapers or whichever radio station they were moonlighting for. Following each match, winner and loser would troop into a small adjoining room to submit to questions from the assembled press. Inevitably the winner would say, "You have to be at your very best" to beat X, Y, or Z, and the loser, appropriately contrite, would allow that the winner "played fantastic today and I made too many unforced errors."

Hangers-on, as well as the occasional player, would pop in for a beer and a gossip. Dapper Ian Doyle, trailing a cloud of after-shave, turned out to be a regular visitor, playing the room, schmoozing with one reporter or another. Reporters, holding plates of lasagna or gluey spaghetti, drifted in and out of an adjoining room where the daily buffet luncheon, which would have been a credit to a Salvation Army soup kitchen, was available, gratis, from Imperial Tobacco. So were complimentary packets of their product; Embassy was obviously not intimidated by fulminating Alex Higgins's pending lawsuit.

Years ago I went on a road trip with the Montreal Canadiens, and I must say that the food on offer in the arena pressrooms in Boston and Buffalo was equally inedible. A French Canadian reporter, noticing that I had declined a bowl of vile chicken soup served out of a bucket, said, "You know, the teams don't have to spend a dime on advertising. We provide them with pages and pages of free coverage, but they treat us like shit."

Tim Burke, then a sports columnist for the Montreal *Gazette*, told me, "Even the goddamn bartenders know we are no better than bums. After a game, you go to the sports bar and naturally they serve the players first, and then—would you believe it?—the referees and linesmen, and finally—if they aren't sucking up to one of the players and don't need to take a break to piss—finally, providing they can spare the time, they will grudgingly take our orders for drinks."

Stephen Hendry, his play no more than adequate, found himself trailing a visibly surprised Stuart Bingham 4-2 in the first
session, but rallied to take it 5-4, finishing with a flourish—
one of his calling-card centuries, a 106 break. However, in the
opening frame of the next session, the seemingly comatose
champion flubbed a cinch green to a balk pocket and retired
to his chair, poker-faced, to watch Bingham deliver a 51 clearance, good enough to level things at 5-5. Only a half-hour later,
an increasingly confident Bingham, hard put to suppress a
smile, pulled ahead 8-5. Even then, knowledgeable observers
didn't doubt that Hendry would ultimately prevail. He did win
the next frame and, like the Arnie Palmer of old, he was now
expected to charge, teaching the lad a lesson he would never
forget: "Hey, I'm Stephen Hendry, and you're not." But an obdurate Bingham wouldn't submit. Clearly playing over his head,
he took the fifteenth frame, capitalizing on a fluked red to make
a 53 break. A break of 87 enabled him to win the seventeenth
frame, eliminating the seven-times world champion 10-7.

Astonishment. Consternation. Say Mark McGwire relies on
a corked bat. Let it be known that Mike Tyson has joined a
Franciscan order. Tell me that Michael Schumacher has resolved to yield in the future, rather than attempt to pass another Formula One driver on the corner of a track. But not
that the master of magic universally recognized as the best
snooker player ever has succumbed to a wet-behind-the-ears
journeyman in the first round of Crucible play.

The headline in the next morning's *Observer* read:

Opening day disaster for title holder
after 300-1 outsider Bingham's stunning victory

## CHAMPION HENDRY BEATEN

"Stuart Bingham, unknown, unheralded and unfancied, was responsible for an opening day shock at the Embassy World Championship in Sheffield," wrote Phil Yates, "when bridging a huge gap in experience, he defeated Stephen Hendry, the title holder. . . ."

Reporters scrambled for the record books. Not since the then dominant Steve Davis was humiliated 10-1 by Tony Knowles in the first round of the 1982 championship had there been such an upset. Hendry had become the fifth returning champion to fall in an initial Crucible round, and the first since Dennis Taylor in 1986.

Bingham—who was now guaranteed a check for a minimum of £19,000, more than double his previous best—said, "I can't describe the feeling when I realized I was over the line. I wasn't sure whether I could keep my head together but I did. As the last few balls were going in I started to feel choked up and there were tears in my eyes."

"Considering it was his first time here," said Hendry, "he's produced a fantastic performance. He was determined to enjoy himself and that served him well. I spent the day trying not to lose instead of trying to win. I didn't play my usual aggressive game, made far too many mistakes and my safety was poor."

Then he retreated to his home in Scotland, pursued by the pensées of Big Daddy Doyle, who blamed Hendry's hitherto trustworthy Powerglide cue for his misadventure. "We feel that Stephen has been hitting the ball too hard and that he has a problem with his cue," he said. "So we will have some wood lopped off the top and the same amount added to the butt." Meanwhile he added a stinger, rebuking his client for playing golf at Gleneagles two weeks earlier. "While Stephen says he has been playing well, I think he has been kidding himself. There is no place for golf before the world championship. It's just not on."

Bingham went out in the second round against Jimmy White, albeit losing by a credible 13-9 to the Crucible veteran. The match was tainted by an incident in the opening frame of the evening session. Bingham missed a brown after a spectator, obviously one of White's many supporters, tossed a piece of chewing gum wrapped in tinfoil, which landed in Bingham's sight line, on the carpet in front of the table. "It got me a bit worried," said Bingham. "I went out there to enjoy it but that distracted me and I couldn't enjoy it. It didn't hit me, but as I walked round the table I saw something out of the corner of my eye. You've got to think some of the crowd are out of order. It's hard, because you're not just playing Jimmy, you're playing them as well."

Many years ago Alexander Woollcott, then drama critic for *The New Yorker*, took James Thurber along to an opening night on Broadway. The play proved to be exceptionally boring, and when the phone rang and rang and rang onstage,

Thurber called out, "Somebody answer it. It could be for me," which broke up the audience. The next day the irate playwright blamed Thurber for the disastrous opening night. Woollcott responded by writing that Thurber was not what was wrong with the play. Similarly, Bingham would have lost to White in any event. The chewing gum was not responsible.

Besting Hendry at the table had to make for a hallelujah day for Bingham, but he struck me, perhaps unreasonably, as a sad case. Somebody who had reached his professional life's zenith at the know-nothing age of twenty-three, the rest likely to be a dying fall. True, his most recent ranking was number thirty-five, a giant step up from ninety-two, but that placement still confined him in the thick of the also-rans who had to qualify for major tournaments. In my mind's eye, I saw him fifty years on, dandling a grandchild on his knee even as he reached for a scrapbook of yellowing newspaper cuttings: "Why, back in the year 2000, I drew Stephen Hendry in the Crucible's first round. Everybody assumed your granddad was a goner, but. . . ."

On the other hand, I could be wrong. He may yet prove to be more than just another one of snookerdom's footnotes.

To be fair to Bingham, Jimmy White's opponent in the Crucible's first round—Billy Snaddon, a thirty-year-old Scot—also complained about the behavior of The Whirlwind's loutish fans during their match, some of them calling out, urging him to miss a pot or make an in-off, the cue ball gliding into a pocket, counting as a foul. "It has nothing to do with Jimmy," said Snaddon, "he's one of the nicest guys on the circuit, but some of those people wanted throwing out. They were all screaming for Jimmy. I don't think anybody out there wanted me to win."

Such is the fans' affection for the so-called People's Champion, who had already taken £3,767,124 at the table but had never won a Crucible title, that some even gathered outside the theater to gawk at his garage-sponsored car, JIMMY WHITE emblazoned on the door.

White, who took out Snaddon 10-7, professed to have had his own problem, a bad case of the flu, in that match. Rising to the defense of his fans, White accused his opponents of talking bullshit, just making excuses. "If some of those players went for a few balls instead of playing safe then they'd get a few fans also. I take chances and the punters like it. It's my style from the first day I played the game and it's the way the people want it. I won't stop."

White was initially posted at 80-2 by the bookies, but he enjoyed so much sentimental support from his legions of admirers that those odds soon shrank to a ludicrous 12-1. "The public do not like White; they adore him," wrote Guy Hodgson in the *Independent,* who then went on to question those loopy 12-1 odds: "Jimmy White at 12-1? This is a man who last won a ranking tournament eight years ago, who last prevailed at any event in June 1993 and who has made it to the final at the Crucible six times and not won the thing. He can't win here. He can't, can he?"

Not according to Simon Barnes, who ventured in the *Times*

that he never would. "He knows it. You can see it in his eyes. Also, you can read a still more fearful thing. He knows that he could have won it, and should have won it."

The true heir of Alex Higgins, White has seen his time come and go. After starting out as a fourteen-year-old, hustling for a few quid in the poolrooms of Tooting, he is now a father of five who has survived testicular cancer and the ministrations of both Gamblers and Alcoholics Anonymous. A onetime bankrupt and still a binge drinker, he is rumored to have squandered £3 million on gambling.

Young Matthew Stevens took out White 13-7 in a quarterfinal. "I missed a very simple black in the seventh and I never really got into it from then on," said White afterwards. "There's no way I'll quit. I still love the game and I love competing. On top form I can win competitions but today I couldn't stay with Matthew. He's definitely world-class and very mature for his age. He shows that with the shots he goes for."

White's loss dropped him out of the magical circle of the top sixteen. In the future, he would have to qualify for tournaments.

Steve Davis is a six-times Crucible champion, winner of seventy-three titles. His skills are now sadly diminished, yet he continues to confound his opponents, or at least some of them, with his foxy play, unnerving more fluent youngsters by constantly slowing the action. He has become snooker's Harold Pinter, a master of meaningful pauses. These cunning tactics certainly rattled twenty-two-year-old Graeme Dott in their first round at the Crucible. Dott trailed the old pro 6-0 when time was called in their first session, though it was incomplete, as it had already lasted three hours and fourteen minutes. A raging Dott adjudged Davis's behavior "scandalous, bordering on cheating." He couldn't believe how slowly Davis was playing. "He was absolutely crawling around the table. I have never seen anyone play as slowly as that. I think it was deliberate and he should be pulled up about it. He was getting down and looking at every angle, even for the break-off. He also went to the toilet between every frame. To my mind the referee should have said something. I'm pretty sure I would have been told off had it been me. It was just so deliberate."

A bemused Davis responded, "I can assure you that I only go to the toilet when I want to empty my bladder." Then, poker-faced, he added, "It's all right for Graeme, he's only in his early twenties. I'm forty-two and that prostate thing kicks in. Every time I went out it was because I needed to pee, simple as that."

His precocious prostate condition notwithstanding, Davis ventured that he had had Dott on the ropes early on and had been slowly banging the nails in. "As Terry Griffiths says, Stephen Hendry tries to steamroller opponents and I try to anesthetize them. That's the way I learned to play this game. Ray Reardon and Cliff Thorburn played that way, it's the way I grew up. You cannot teach an old dog new tricks."

World number-one player John Higgins, the sly old pisser's

next opponent, rose to Davis's defense. "I was only five," he said, "when Steve won his first world championship, and he's a player I've always enjoyed watching. I think Graeme was a bit despondent at losing. I'm sure, now that he's back home, he'll realize that Steve played like he did to have a better chance of beating him. If he had come out and attacked, that would have suited Graeme a lot more."

Then, having made nice, he went on to beat the molasses-slow Davis 13-11, intimidating him with clearances of 141, 137, and 127 en route.

Hendry was not the Crucible's only falling star. Ronnie O'Sullivan was also taken out in a first round, 10-9, done in by yet another Crucible rookie, twenty-one-year-old David Gray, rated number sixty. *Snooker Scene* hailed their opening session, after which O'Sullivan led 5-4, as "one of the highest quality sessions of this, or for that matter any other Embassy World Championship."

Snooker-beat reporters, like baseball scribes, are ever eager to pounce on records, no matter how arcane. So all of them noted that O'Sullivan had become only the second player, after John Higgins in 1998, to record three centuries in as many frames at the Crucible.

Possibly they should look into another phenomenon, the contradictory effect of a parent's demise on a player's performance. David Gray, deeply affected by the death of his father two years earlier, suffered a spell, he said, "when my game was weak but now I feel more confident."

On the other hand, Joe Swail, following his 13-12 defeat of John Parrott in a second round, was tearful. "All I could think of was Mum," he said, "Josephine, who died of cancer two years ago at the age of fifty-seven. She was and still is my inspiration. She was always behind me and in a funny way this made me realize not to throw away the talent I had."

Of course, much earlier, Kirk Stevens was willing to blab to the tabloids—providing they were willing to pay—about how his mother's murder had affected him. And the imprisonment of Ronnie O'Sullivan's dad on a murder charge still figures prominently in his continuing psychodrama. But I shouldn't be too harsh on snooker players in our degraded age, when reticence has become rare and a paid-for confessional is the happy rule: former cabinet ministers, movie stars, and athletes, as well as that notorious former lover of Diana, Princess of Wales, jostling each other in their rush to bleed in public, so long as the price is right.

The premature elimination of fan favorites Jimmy White and Ronnie O'Sullivan let a good deal of air out of the Crucible balloon. Any player I spoke to who was not going to win himself was pulling for Jimmy White to take the title, as were so many of the fans. And every time O'Sullivan stepped up to the table there was the promise of dazzling play. Maybe a lightning-quick 147. O'Sullivan effortlessly created the kind of buzz that the Montreal Canadiens' Guy Lafleur, in his prime, could manage by merely leaping over the boards to glide onto the ice. However, the early loss of Hendry, albeit astonishing, was not widely regretted. Increasingly he came to the table as if enduring another gloomy day at the office.

A week later, I met a subdued Hendry for lunch at Gleneagles, where he golfs regularly. "I work inside most of the year," he said. "I can't tell you what a pleasure it is to be outdoors. When I was seventeen or eighteen, you couldn't get me away from the practice table—that's all I cared about. But nowadays five or six hours of daily practice can be a chore."

Once, years ago, I was invited to Pete Rose's home in an affluent Cincinnati suburb. He promptly escorted me into the basement for a tour of his very own Pete Rose Museum. Trophies here, there, and everywhere. Plaques. Paintings of the great man. The bat he had used to connect for his three-thousandth hit. A scorecard establishing that he had hit safely in his thirty-seventh consecutive game. The cap he had worn in a World Series. A proud Gordie Howe once led me through a similar room in Hartford, celebrating his achievements on and off the ice. Mounted on only one wall were The Victors Award, The American Academy of Achievement Golden Plate Award, The American Captain of Achievement Award. "I understand you write novels," said Howe.

"Yes."

"There must be a good market for them. You see them on racks in all the supermarkets now."

Happily, Hendry does not maintain a trophy room in his home. His many tournament tchotchkes are held for him at Spencer's Leisure and Snooker Club, in Stirling, where he practices. Jealous of his privacy, he will not allow anybody to interview Mandy, his pretty blond wife, an accomplished show jumper. He once told a reporter, "Mandy hates snooker. I'll walk through the door and she won't allow me to mention it."

This struck me as rank ingratitude, considering that he had already brought home better than six million quid from those tables. "But doesn't she watch you on TV when you're playing?"

"Not if there's something better on another channel. 'Coronation Street' or 'Brookside.'"

"Have you been following Crucible play on TV?"

"I did my best to avoid it. What happened was very disappointing. I had begun to feel the title belonged to me."

"Ian Doyle has quoted you as saying that Ronnie O'Sullivan has more talent in his fingertips than the rest of you have in your entire bodies."

"I didn't include myself in that estimate. I still believe I am the most talented."

Most of the multimillionaire snooker players favor flash sports cars, but not Hendry. A grateful sponsor once made him a gift of a Ferrari 348, and another time he was presented with a Bentley Continental. He traded them both in and now drives a BMW. Even so, he is an ardent Formula One fan and will stay up until three a.m. to catch a race live from Australia or Japan.

"Have you any interest in politics?"

"No."

"Don't you vote?"

"No."

"I once read somewhere that you intended to retire at thirty, but now you're thirty-one and still playing."

He shrugged.

"Some observers have charged that you've lost your appetite for the game."

"I'd like to play for another four or five years. I want to win the world championship again."

But would he hang in there, long past his prime, like Steve Davis, who had just slipped out of the top sixteen in the rankings?

"If there's no success at the table, there can be no enjoyment. Only five years ago I could count on winning five or six tournaments a season, but now the competition is tougher. It's very hard. If I ever slipped out of the top four in the rankings, I might think again about continuing to play."

"And then what?"

"I'd like to be a commentator."

Meanwhile, he added, his money was being wisely invested for him by Papa Doyle.

On off-days between matches, the affable Mark Williams, world number one and easily the most relaxed of the contenders, would often drift into the pressroom for a beer and a chat with John Dee of the *Telegraph*.

Slowly, surely, Williams worked his passage through the seventeen-day ordeal in Sheffield. He took out Crucible rookie John Read 10-4 in his opening round, winning five frames in the second session in a mere sixty-nine minutes. He was put to a more severe test in his second round, but finally prevailed 13-9 over Drew Henry. Next he coasted to a 13-5 win over Fergal O'Brien in a quarter-final. He encountered stiffer opposition in his semifinal in the shape of John Higgins, who had already seen him off in ten of their previous thirteen meetings. At one point he trailed 15-11, Higgins requiring only two of the remaining possible nine frames to win. But Williams took the next six and Higgins had to be satisfied with a £70,000 consolation check. *Snooker Scene* applauded this contest: "Anyone who witnessed last year's Crucible semifinal involving these same protagonists would find it difficult to believe that the re-match could possibly be better but, during the first session, 92 minutes of magnificent, largely one chance Snooker, Higgins constructed six breaks of over 40, while Williams had three half centuries and a century."

Going through my own notes again months later, I was reminded of how seventeen days of clicking snooker balls, afternoon and evening, was a bit much, even for a fan like me. I had begun to long for home, if not for "Coronation Street" or "Brookside," like Mandy. I was also reminded of how jubilant I was to see disagreeable Stephen Lee lose 13-8 to Fergal O'Brien in a second round. "Apart from his 126 break in the tenth frame," noted *Snooker Scene*, "it was a nightmare session for last year's Grand Prix champion, who was undoubtedly handicapped by a defective tip he intended to replace after the match, regardless of the result."

Excuses, excuses. Years ago the Montreal *Gazette*'s uncommonly literate sports columnist Dink Carroll told me a story about a onetime ace but hard-luck pitcher for our Triple "A" Montreal Royals. Dropping a well-pitched game 2-0, he would complain about his lack of support at the plate. Losing another 5-4, he would whine about a harmless fly ball that had dropped for a double in left field. Or point out that the short-stop had muffed an easy grounder, costing two runs. Weary of his excuses, the veteran catcher took him aside and told him, "In this game, bubba, either you do or you don't. So shettup."

I was truly sorry to see Hendry expire so early, because I readily identified with an "aging" player who had possibly hung in for one tournament too many, even as I and other old writers usually scribble one novel too many. But throughout, I was impressed by Mark Williams's easygoing nature. I suspected that he knew there was more to life than what was available on the green baize. Alone among the contestants, I felt, if he failed in the final, he would have another beer and not lose a night's sleep.

Happily, the two-day all-Welsh final, with Williams taking on his chum Matthew Stevens, turned out to be truly exciting. STEVENS FORGETS OLD FRIENDSHIP TO GIVE WELSH RIVAL THE SLIP, wrote John Dee in the *Telegraph*, as Stevens led 10-6 at the end of the first day's play. "We're the best of mates," said Stevens, "but we won't be for two days here. It's great, though, that whoever wins means the title is going back to Wales."

The second day's play belonged to the coal miner's son, who ultimately won the squeaker 18-16. WILLIAMS CROWNED

PRINCE OF WALES, wrote Phil Yates in the *Times*: "Mark Williams, seemingly heading for his second crushing Crucible disappointment in as many years, last night produced a recovery as spirited as it was memorable. . . ."

His win brought the record-keepers out of the woodwork. Williams was the first left-hander and only the third Welshman to win the title, worth £240,000—a notable improvement on the £6 10s the first champion, Joe Davis, had taken home in 1927, even if you take inflation into account. Williams was also the third player to make the U.K. and world championship double in the same season, following Steve Davis twice and Hendry three times. He was crowned champion on Sunday May 1, yet another Doyle client who had played hooky on the Gleneagles golf course two weeks prior to the Crucible test. Afterwards, he left a jokey message on his mate Hendry's answering machine: "It's official. I'm the number one now—up yours."

Mark Williams's dad was too tense to watch the final. "I went for a walk outside," he told John Dee. "I couldn't bear it but Mark has done us proud. It doesn't seem that long ago that I took him to a club near home. I went for a couple of pints and he played for the first time. He was about twelve and he was damn good at the game. He played pool for Gwent County, you know."

Williams's triumph was popular with his peers and the fans. It was especially popular with his fellow Welshman Kevin Bohn, a factory worker. Bohn had first seen the then fourteen-year-old Williams play at a junior amateur event in

1989, and he had immediately forked over £140 to a book-maker, wagering, at odds of 300-1, that Williams would win the world title before 2001.

Bohn saw his faith rewarded with a check for £42,000.

# — *Postscript* —

SHORTLY after Mark Williams won the Crucible title, Florence and I, as was our habit, quit London and returned to our cottage on Lake Memphremagog in time to enjoy a second spring, daffodils risking the cold night air and mounds of snow still shrinking on our driveway. Once again a snooker table of my own was available, but—having seen the masters at play, embarrassed by my ineptitude—it was weeks before I dared to pick up my cue again.

We were back in our winter quarters in London the following mid-November, enabling me to catch up on the snooker scene.

Brusque wannabe modernizer of snookerdom Peter Middleton had endured a rough spring and summer. In May he had resigned as chairman of Luton Airport. Stelios Hajiloannou, chairman of Easyjet, who was obviously not a fan, said that Middleton wanted to run things, but Barclay's, which owned 60 percent of Luton, saw things differently from Middleton. Hajiloannou told the *Independent*, "The first time

I met him he stormed out of the room. We then exchanged some very angry letters. He said: 'I used to run Lloyd's when it was turning over so many billions in fees. I used to run Salomon Brothers when it was turning over so many billions on the trading floor and I'm not going to be intimidated by you and your little company.'"

Liberated from Luton, Middleton (representing Nomura, a Japanese financial house) was able to concentrate on what would turn out to be his unsuccessful bid for the Millennium Dome. Come summer, Rabbi Everton took umbrage in one of his *Snooker Scene* tractates, noting, "Snooker folk began to question the desirability of [Middleton] continuing at WPBSA, where he was beginning to outlive the favourable first impressions he had created." He hadn't helped his cause by canceling his appearance at one board meeting on only a few minutes' notice. Furthermore, he had made such radical staff cuts in the association's Bristol head office that there were suddenly hardly enough knowledgeable hands left to mind the shop. In August Middleton resigned his two-days-a-week, £50,000-a-year stint as chief executive of the WPBSA. An official statement praised Middleton's work in "reconstructing the company and helping to put it on a sound financial footing" but it failed to back up this accolade with any numbers. What is known is that Middleton had failed to deliver promised new sponsorships, notably an Internet rights deal with Ian Doyle's The Sportsmasters Network (TSN) said to be worth £3.3 million.

Sole surviving Canadian on the circuit, troubled Alain

Robidoux had learned to live with his new cue. Rated a lowly number ninety-nine, he got as far as a third qualifying round for the Grand Prix at Telford but didn't make it to the main event. In the newly organized Seniors' Circuit, Kirk Stevens was eliminated in the first round of the inaugural Seniors' Masters, at the Royal Automobile Club in London in May, but Cliff Thorburn reached the final only to be beaten by the redoubtable Willie Thorne. Thorburn settled for £7,500 for his trouble.

Suffering slamming doors, screaming kids, and the racket from a racing game in an adjoining arcade, Jimmy White nevertheless won his first title in six years at a holiday camp in Prestatyn in May. Only a few months later White and Steve Davis, no longer rated among the elite sixteen, both failed to qualify for the £440,000 Regal Welsh Open.

In June Ronnie O'Sullivan, dubbed the greatest natural talent the game had ever known, proved once again that uneasy lies the noggin beneath the crown. He was charged with declining an invitation for a breath, blood, or urine test after being stopped by the police on suspicion of driving under the influence of drink. O'Sullivan's Porsche was trailed by an MGF sports car. He and a girl got out of the Porsche, and two spare girls, one wearing only a bathrobe, got out of the MGF. Asked to comment, Ian Doyle, bless him, said, "I don't know why she was wearing a bathrobe." But the answer was obvious to me. I've been around. The poor girl's boiler had broken down, and the gallant O'Sullivan was leading her to a place where she could bathe.

In July, O'Sullivan booked into the Priory Clinic, in Roe-
hampton, for five weeks, to be treated for drug addiction. Ian
Doyle refused to confirm or deny a *News of the World* allega-
tion that the drug at issue was cocaine. "It came as a shock to
all of us," he said, "that Ronnie had checked into the Priory.
This is not the kind of news you want to hear about any
player, but he has been man enough to admit he has a serious
problem and has done something about it for himself. The
word I'm getting is that he is progressing well and that, if he's
left alone and allowed to recover in his own time, he'll be back
for the new season."

Emerging from the clinic, O'Sullivan said, "I've been
through a lot of stuff in the past few months, but I've got my
life in order and the public will see a different side of me."
Then he added that winning tournaments was gratifying, but
that he also longed "to feel happy inside"—without, I take it,
the benefit of happy dust.

REVITALISED O'SULLIVAN MAKES A FLYING START
TO NEW SEASON, wrote Everton in the October *Snooker
Scene*, and he was bang on. For starters, O'Sullivan took
Hendry and Mark Williams in the last two rounds to win the
£100,000 first prize in the Champions Cup at Brighton. Next
he won the Regal Scottish Masters and from there he moved
on to Shenzhen to retain his China Open title. This put him
well ahead in the money list, with £280,000 netted in three
tournaments. However, his personal psychodrama continued.
Following his triumph in China, he told a press conference
that he felt frustrated and drained: "Nothing really matters to

me, apart from getting my life back in order."

Stephen Hendry's cue suffered major surgery before the new season began but, all the same, he continued to struggle. Cue doctor Lawrie Annandale took an inch and a half off the top, two inches off the bottom, and then put the total back on the bottom end. Practicing with the new cue, Hendry said, "You can't really tell it's changed when I'm playing."

At the Liverpool Victoria U.K. Championship at Bournemouth International Centre, in November, two former world champions who had known better days, Hendry and Steve Davis, met in a sixth-round encounter. In spite of mistakes, Hendry managed an unconvincing win over Davis. "There was some horrendous stuff," he allowed afterwards. "To say there's thirteen world titles between us, you wouldn't have thought there were thirteen local club championships."

Hendry endeared himself to me by eliminating Stephen Lee 9-8 in another round, but he came a cropper in a semifinal, losing 9-4 to his former practice partner, John Higgins, who went on to win the title.

Ian Doyle once told me that Hendry was even more famous in China than he was in the U.K., that he had had to be rescued by security police, taking refuge in the media center after he was mobbed by autograph hunters following his 5-2 defeat of Pete Ebdon in the second round of the China Open in the Mission Hills club in Shenzhen. In what was really a grudge match, Hendry, in vintage form, managed clearances of 121, 106, 94, 81, and 60. "That was the best I've played all season," he said, "but I was really psyched up for the match—

I wish I played like that against everyone else."

Hendry beat Alan McManus 5-2 in the next round, and the *Telegraph*'s John Dee, anticipating, declared that this "means that the 31-year-old Scot remains on course for becoming the first player to win ranking titles in three different decades, the 1980s, 1990s and 2000s." But it was not to be, at least not yet, because title-bound Ronnie O'Sullivan beat him in the semifinal.

As of January 2001, Hendry had not won a ranking title for sixteen months. He slid to number four in the rankings.

# ~ *Envoi* ~

IN AN OTHERWISE generous review of my most recent novel, *Barney's Version*, that appeared in the London *Spectator*, Francis King had one caveat. Noting the sharpness of protagonist Barney Panofsky's intelligence and the breadth of his culture, he doubted that he could also be a sports nut. "Would such a man, obsessed with ice hockey, be able to pronounce with such authority on topics as diverse as the descriptive passages in the novels of P. D. James, *Pygmalion* as play, musical and film, the pornography published by Maurice Girodias's Olympic Press and Dr. Johnson's *The Vanity of Human Wishes*?—rather strains credulity."

But North American literary men in general, and the Jewish writers among them in particular, have always been obsessed by sports. We acquire the enthusiasm as kids and carry it with us into middle age and beyond, adjudging it far more enjoyable than lots of other baggage we still lug around. Arguably, we settled for writing, a sissy's game, because we couldn't "float like a butterfly and sting like a bee," pitch a curveball, catch, deke, score a touchdown.

"Why did football bring me so to life?" wrote Frederick Exley in *A Fan's Notes*.

> Part of it was my feeling that football was an island of directness in a world of circumspection. In football a man was asked to do a difficult and brutal job, and either he did it or got out. There was nothing rhetorical or vague about it; I chose to believe that it was not unlike the jobs which all men, in some sunnier past, had been called upon to do. It smacked of something old, something traditional, something unclouded by legerdemain and subterfuge. It had that kind of power over me, drawing me back with the force of something known, scarcely remembered, elusive as integrity—perhaps it was no more than the force of a forgotten childhood. Whatever it was, I gave myself up to the Giants utterly. The recompense I gained was the feeling of being alive.

George Plimpton, acting out our fantasies, did get to pitch in Yankee Stadium while a bona fide intellectual, Robert Silvers, editor of *The New York Review of Books*, sat in the stands marking a scorecard. Plimpton next trained with the Detroit Lions, and wrote engaging books about both his experiences. He also wanted to try his hand at tending the nets of the Detroit Red Wings, but, he told me, he was refused permission by the coach, who warned him, "The puck is mindless."

And, he might have added, can come zinging in on a goalie at one hundred miles per hour. However, Plimpton did eventually go on to tend goal and write *Open Net*.

Norman Mailer got to spar with both Archie Moore and José Torres. And, in perhaps the most famous boxing match in literary history, Morley Callaghan fought Ernest Hemingway in a Paris gym in the twenties, Scott Fitzgerald acting as timekeeper. In his memoir, *That Summer in Paris*, Callaghan claimed that he had knocked Hemingway down only after Papa had both startled and insulted him by spitting in his face. The embarrassed Hemingway, on the other hand, accused the duplicitous Fitzgerald of allowing the round to go beyond three minutes, without which there would have been no knockdown. He also complained that Callaghan, in search of publicity, had passed on news of Hemingway's humiliation to a New York newspaper gossip columnist, but Callaghan denied the story.

Sport weighs heavily on the American literary man's psyche. Back in the seventies, when I once met Irwin Shaw for drinks in the Polo Lounge, in Beverly Hills, he was still touchy about being patronized by the Jewish literary mafia, the *Commentary* intelligentsia rating him below the trinity of Bellow, Malamud, and Roth. "They could never forgive me for being such a good football player," he said.

North American men of letters, incidentally, are not the only literary sports nutters. Albert Camus, for one, liked to brag about his prowess on the soccer pitch. However, if we are sports-obsessed, at least we don't attempt to dignify our boyish enthusiasms with intellectual gibberish. Were you aware, for instance, that the soccer ball is a symbol of saint-hood? Or that goalkeepers are patriarchal figures with roots deep in the culture of European Christendom? Such, in any event, were the conclusions reached by Günter Gebauer, professor of philosophy at the Institute of Sport in Berlin, speaking at Cité Philo, a month-long philosophy festival that took place late in 2000 at Lens, near Lille, in northern France. Ruminating on the meaning of the soccer ball, Herr Gebauer said, "It is mistreated in the most vile fashion . . . but it returns to your feet and is cherished and loved. This is like the saint who is thrown out of town and comes back to conquer people's hearts."

He also had some original thoughts on the goal and goalkeeper. "They are bound up with intrinsically European values, where our house is our castle and the source of pride and honor. We guard it against intrusion, just as a goal-keeper guards his goal. Scoring is like penetrating into a stranger's house, burning his belongings or raping his wife and daughter."

Then, as no conference of European intellectuals would be complete without its anti-American dig, he added, "In the U.S. the attachment to notions of honor and pride are far less strong, which no doubt explains why there is no goal or goal-keeper in their version of football."

Never mind that the American corruption of soccer does include a goal or touchdown line, coveted by rapists, but what about ice hockey? My all-time favorite hockey goalie, Gump

Worsley, also a philosopher of sorts, once tended the nets for the hapless New York Rangers.

"Which team gives you the most trouble?" a reporter once asked.

"The Rangers," he said.

Another professor of philosophy at Cité Philo, Jean-Michel Salanskis, ventured that soccer was not for the mentally disadvantaged. "Wherever you go in the world," he said, "people talk about soccer in terms of theories. There is the theory of the playmaker, the theory of the counterattack, the theory of the three-man defense, and so on." Such capacity for abstract thought, he suggested, made every fan a potential philosopher.

Obviously he had never been to a British soccer match, the riot police and ambulances in attendance, the philosophers in the stands, many of them with shaven heads, heaving bananas at the black players, pissing against the nearest wall or even where they sat; I remember an intimidating puddle once forming at my feet in the row immediately below them.

When I was a child, it was sport that first enabled me to grasp that the adult world was suspect. Tainted by lies and betrayals. This insight came about when I discovered that our home baseball team, the Triple "A" Montreal Royals, which I was enjoined to cheer for, was in fact made up of strangers, hired hands, most of them American southerners who were long gone once the season was over and had never been tested by a punishing Montreal winter. Only during the darkest days of the Second

World War, when deprivation was the unhappy rule—coffee and sugar and gasoline all rationed, American comic books temporarily unavailable, one-armed Pete Gray toiling in the Toronto Maple Leafs' outfield—only then did French Canadian players off the local sandlots briefly play for the Royals: Stan Bréard at *arrêt-court*, Roland Gladu at *troisième but,* and Jean-Pierre Roy at *lanceur.* A few years later my bunch could root for a Jewish player, outfielder Kermit Kitman, who eventually settled in Montreal, ending up in the schmatte trade. When he was with the Royals, Kitman was paid $650 monthly for six months of the year, a bonanza enriched by $3 a day meal money on the road. Kitman told me, "As a Jewish boy, I could eat on that money and maybe even save a little in those days. The Gentile players had enough left over for beer and cigarettes."

My disenchantment with the baseball Royals, counterfeit hometowners, didn't matter as soon as I discovered that I could give my unqualified love to the Montreal Canadiens, *nos glorieux*, then a team unique in sport because most of its star performers were Quebecers born and bred, many of whom had to drive beer trucks or take construction jobs in summer in order to make ends meet. I speak of the incomparable Richard brothers, Maurice and Henri; goalie Jacques Plante, who knitted between periods; and Doug Harvey, universally acknowledged as the outstanding defenseman of his time, who never was paid more than $15,000 a season, and in his last boozy days earned his beer money sharpening skates in his brother's sports shop, for kids who had no idea who he was. There were two great Montreal teams. The greatest, certainly, was the Canadiens club that won the Stanley Cup for the fifth consecutive year in 1959–60; Jean Béliveau, Dickie Moore, Bernie "Boom Boom" Geoffrion, Henri Richard and an aging Maurice "The Rocket" Richard up front, Doug Harvey minding the blue line, and Jacques Plante in the nets. The second great Canadiens team—led by Guy Lafleur, Yvan Cournoyer, Jacques Lemaire, Guy Lapointe, Serge Savard, and Larry Robinson, with Ken Dryden in the nets—won its fourth Stanley Cup in a row in 1979. And only because they had performed with such panache were we willing to forgive Robinson and Dryden for being renegade Anglos from Ontario.

I turned then, as I turn now, to the sports pages first in my morning newspaper, unlike Frederick Exley, who would begin by reading the book review and entertainment sections: "Finally I turned to the sports sections. Even then I did not begin reading about the Giants. I was like a child who, having been given a box of chocolates, eats the jellies and nuts first and saves the creamy caramels till last. I read about golf in Scotland, surf-boarding in Oahu, football as Harvard imagines it played, and deep-sea fishing in Mexico. Only then did I turn to the Giants. . . ."

In the forties it was radio that was our primary source of sports news. Saturday nights we usually tuned in to the overexcited Foster Hewitt on "Hockey Night in Canada." Like millions of others on the night of June 18, 1941, we huddled round our RCA Victor radio to listen to the broadcast from the Polo Grounds in New York, as former light heavyweight champion Billy Conn took on the incomparable Joe Louis.

The Brown Bomber, patronizingly described again and again as "a credit to his people," also qualified as a Jewish hero, ever since he had redeemed our kind by knocking out Max Schmeling in their second meeting. Conn, a clever boxer, was ahead on points after twelve rounds, but in the thirteenth he foolishly stood toe-to-toe with Louis, intent on flattening him. Instead, Louis knocked him out at 2:52 of the thirteenth.

My heart went out, however grudgingly, to the Brooklyn Dodgers, if only because so many of their players had served their apprenticeship with our Montreal Royals, the organization's number-one farm team. Not only did we get to delight in the legendary Jackie Robinson tormenting pitchers in Delormier Downs, a constant threat to pilfer a base, but we also got to watch the young Duke Snider, Carl Furillo, Roy Campanella, Ralph Branca, Carl Erskine, and Don Newcombe. One autumn afternoon I joined a concerned knot of fans outside Jack and Moe's barbershop to listen to the radio broadcast of the infamous World Series game wherein catcher Mickey Owen dropped that third strike, enabling the dreaded Yankees to trample the jinxed Dodgers yet again.

When we were St. Urbain Street urchins, six-foot-four Hank Greenberg—the Detroit Tigers' first baseman who hit 313 home runs in a career that was interrupted by four years of military service in the Second World War—was our hero. Proof positive that not all Jews were necessarily short, good at chess, but unable to swing a bat. In 1934 Greenberg, a nonobservant Jew, decided it wouldn't be proper for him to play in a World Series game on Yom Kippur, and became the subject of a poem of sorts by Edgar A. Guest, the last stanza of which reads:

> Come Yom Kippur—holy fast world wide
> > over the Jew—
> And Hank Greenberg to his teaching and the
> > old tradition true
> Spent his day among his people and he didn't
> > come to play.
> Said Murphy to Mulrooney, "We shall lose
> > the game today!
> We shall miss him in the infield and shall
> > miss him at the bat,
> But he's true to his religion—and I honor him
> > for that!"

Greenberg is one of only two Jewish players in the Baseball Hall of Fame, the other being Sandy Koufax, who also refused to play on Yom Kippur.

Numbering high among my most cherished sports memories is the night in the sixties, in New York, when Ted Solotaroff, then an editor at *Commentary* magazine, took me to the Polo Grounds to watch Sandy Koufax pitch a two-hitter. He went nine innings, of course, but those were the days when a starter was expected to go nine, or at least eight, rather than to be hugged by his teammates if he managed six, to be followed on the mound by a succession of multi-millionaire holders and closers.

Although I spent some twenty years in England, I could

never—unlike our children, who were brought up there—acquire a taste for soccer or cricket. So I can appreciate that most Englishmen of my acquaintance have no interest in ice hockey and consider baseball a bore. "Isn't that the game," I have been asked more than once, "that grown men play in their pajamas?"

The absurdity of sport in general, American football in particular, to people who weren't brought up on our games, was once illuminated for me by the Canadian writer and broadcaster Peter Gzowski. Gzowski, a frequent traveler to the Arctic, told me that as far as the Inuit were concerned, football was funnier than any sitcom available on TV. They would gather round a set in Inuvik, falling about with laughter at the sight of the players in their outlandish gear, especially savoring the spectacle of them testing their armor on the sidelines, banging into each other like caribou in heat.

Not only do American literary guys tend to be obsessed by sport, but many have written with distinction about games. George Plimpton, already mentioned, has hardly ever written about anything else. A baseball game between yeshiva students and goy boys was crucial to Chaim Potok's novel *The Chosen*. Bernard Malamud and Philip Roth have both had their tickets punched with baseball novels: *The Natural* and *Our Gang*. Saul Bellow has yet to oblige, but in his most recent novel, *Ravelstein*, the imposing intellectual protagonist is a sports nut, an avid fan of both the Chicago Cubs and the Chicago basketball Bulls. I will also include my own modest contribution here: a long set piece in my novel *St. Urbain's Horseman*, about a baseball game played by blacklisted expatriate American filmmakers on Hampstead Heath in the sixties. That compelling but sadly underrated laureate of Boston low life, the novelist George Higgins, wrote a fine tribute to his sad love affair with the Boston Red Sox; and Richard Ford, who once labored for *Sports Illustrated*, contributed his splendid novel *The Sportswriter*:

> Athletes, by and large, are people who are happy to let their actions speak for them, happy to be what they do. As a result, when you talk to an athlete, as I do all the time in locker rooms, in hotel coffee shops and hallways, standing beside expensive automobiles—even if he's paying no attention to you at all, which is very often the case—he's never likely to feel the least bit divided, or alienated, or one ounce of existential dread. . . . Years of athletic training teach him this: the necessity of relinquishing doubt and ambiguity and self-inquiry in favor of a pleasant self-championing one-dimensionality which has instant rewards in sports. You can even ruin everything with athletes simply by speaking to them in your own everyday voice, a voice possibly full of contingency and speculation. It will scare them to death by demonstrating that the world—where they often don't do too well and sometimes fall into depressions and financial imbroglios and worse once their careers

are over—is complexer than what their training has prepared them for.

Robert Coover wrote one of the most original baseball novels I know of, *The Universal Baseball Association, Inc.* But the classic baseball novel, first published in 1916 and happily still in print, as fresh and acute as ever, is Ring Lardner's *You Know Me Al*—much admired, as unlikely as it seems, by Virginia Woolf, who justifiably accounted Lardner a talent of a remarkable order.

Boxing, above all, has attracted the attention of literary men in England as well as America. Dr. Johnson, Swift, Pope, and Hazlitt have all had their considerable say. In America Jack London, James Farrell, Nelson Algren, John O'Hara, Ring Lardner, Hemingway, Irwin Shaw, Budd Schulberg, Norman Mailer, and Wilfrid Sheed have all written about the sport. So have W. C. Heinz and Ted Hoagland, and of course there is Leonard Gardner's wonderful novel *Fat City*.

Not only guys have pronounced on what Pierce Egan dubbed "the sweet science," but also Joyce Carol Oates. Her erudite *On Boxing* must be the only book about the game that refers, *en passant*, to Petronius, Thorstein Veblen, Santayana, Yeats, Beckett, Ionesco, Emily Dickinson, and both William and Henry James, among others. Joyce Carol Oates was introduced to boxing in the early fifties when her father first took her to a Golden Gloves tournament in Buffalo, New York. Happily, in her original if somewhat eccentric take on the game she does pay tribute, as is only proper, to the great Pierce Egan, author of the classic *Boxiana, or, Sketches of Ancient and Modern Pugilism,* acknowledging that his prose was as wittily nuanced as that of Defoe, Swift, and Pope. However, she finds herself "uneasily alone" in being scornful of A. J. Liebling, a journalist whose boxing writing I cherish. She dislikes Liebling

> for his relentless jokey, condescending, and occasionally racist attitude toward his subject. Perhaps because it was originally published in *The New Yorker* in the early 1950s *The Sweet Science: Boxing and Boxiana—a Ringside View* is a peculiarly self-conscious assemblage of pieces, arch, broad in humor, rather like a situation comedy in which boxers are "characters" depicted for our amusement. Liebling is even uncertain about such champions as Louis, Marciano, and Robinson—should one revere or mock? And he is pitiless when writing about "Hurricane" Jackson, a black boxer cruelly called an animal, an "it," because of his poor boxing skills and what Liebling considers his mental inferiority.

Obviously Ms. Oates does not consider mental inferiority to be the case with Mike Tyson, with whom she spent considerable time. Astonishingly, she adjudges Tyson "clearly thoughtful, intelligent, introspective; yet at the same time—or nearly the same time—he is a 'killer' in the ring. That he is one of the most warmly affectionate persons, yet at the same time—or nearly—a machine for hitting 'sledgehammer' blows."

Cornerman Teddy Atlas, the subject of a *New Yorker* profile by David Remnick, took a different view of Tyson. Atlas, a protégé of Cus D'Amato, helped to train Tyson in Catskill when the boxer was still a teenager. D'Amato, who realized he had a future world champion on his hands, made excuses for the teenage Tyson when he got into trouble in school for threatening teachers or harassing girls, and that, wrote Remnick, was often. Atlas was married to a local girl called Elaine.

"One day in 1982, Atlas came home and saw Elaine and her eleven-year-old sister sitting at the kitchen table crying. They told Atlas that Tyson, who was then sixteen, had come on to the girl, had touched her, demanding things from her, sexual things. Atlas left the apartment in a rage."

He acquired a .38 revolver from a nightclub owner in town, made sure it was loaded, and confronted Tyson in an alley outside the gym, jamming the gun hard into his ear.

"I said, 'You piece of shit! You piece of shit! Don't you *ever* put your hands on my family, I will kill you. Do you understand this?' If he so much as smiled, if he would have said no, I would have killed him. And I would have lived with that. I'm not saying that's right, but at that time that's what it was for me. When I wasn't sure how to save his life, how to give him a chance, I pulled the gun away from his ear and pulled the trigger. I fired. At that moment he knew. He got very weak. I could see that in his eyes. . . . His ear was probably ringing pretty hard and he fell backward a little. . . . Cus had never let Tyson know that the things he was doing to people were real. I was letting him know."

Be that as it may, Joyce Carol Oates won me over with a fetching analogy:

"The artist senses some kinship, however oblique and one-sided, with the professional boxer in this matter of training. This fanatic subordination of the self in terms of a wished-for destiny. One might compare the time-bound public spectacle of the boxing match (which could be as brief as an ignominious forty-five seconds—the record for a title fight!) with the publication of a writer's book. That which is 'public' is but the final stage in a protracted, arduous, grueling, and frequently despairing period of preparation."

And this, she ventures, may be one of the reasons for the habitual attraction of serious writers to boxing.

John Updike, that readiest of writers, has pronounced adoringly about golf both in incidental pieces and in his Rabbit Angstrom novels. "Like a religion," he wrote in *Golf Dreams*, a collection of his golf pieces, "a game seeks to codify and lighten life. Played earnestly enough (spectatorship being merely a degenerate form of playing), a game can gather to itself awesome dimensions of subtlety and transcendental significance. Consult George Steiner's hymn to the fathomless wonder of chess, or Roger Angell's startlingly intense meditations upon the time-stopping, mathematical beauty of baseball. Some sports, surely, are more religious than others; ice hockey, fervent though its devotees, retains a dross of brutal messiness. . . ."

In common, I should have thought, with Islam, Christianity, and Judaism. Or, conversely, hockey is just the ticket for sports agnostics like me.

I am, incidentally, not the only scribbler to write about contests on the green baize. Pushkin, Jane Austen, Dickens, Thackeray, George Eliot, Conrad, and Dostoyevsky all managed to squeeze a description of a billiards game into their work. *Byrne's Book of Great Pool Stories*, a lively anthology edited by Robert Byrne, included billiard stories by Tolstoi, Alphonse Daudet, Saki, Wallace Stegner, William Sansom, and Stephen Leacock, among others. It also features snooker encounters by William Harrison, the Canadian Ken Mitchell, and Booker Prize winner James Kelman. Before they became estranged, Martin Amis and Julian Barnes used to play together regularly. And I can testify that a talented young writer, Emma Richler, is constantly improving her cue work.

Over the years, unable to act out my fantasies like George Plimpton, I have all the same, on assignment for various magazines, been able to accompany the Montreal Canadiens on a road trip, shooting the breeze with Guy Lafleur and playing poker with Toe Blake and others on the coaching staff. I have also got to hang out with Pete Rose and Johnny Bench in Cincinnati, and I once spent some time with the Edmonton Oilers when Wayne Gretzky was still with them. Gretzky, his immense skills undeniable, has to be one of the most boring men I ever met, inclined to talk about himself in the third person. To come clean, neither was the far more appealing Stephen Hendry the wittiest of luncheon companions. But, to

be fair, Gore Vidal hasn't registered fifty hat tricks, and neither has he ever scored a maximum.

As the truly gifted Hendry continues to play erratically, I
would like to remind him that the great Jack Nicklaus, long
after he was written off by golf writers, came back to win another Masters at Augusta, Georgia, at the age of forty-six, in
1986. And so, forearmed with my pacifiers (a ten-pack of
Davidoff's Demi-Tasse cigarillos, a plentiful supply of cashews,
a bowl of cherry tomatoes, a bottle of the Macallan, and another of Highland Spring mineral water), I will be watching
the Embassy World Championship on TV this spring, pulling
for Hendry to confound us and win his eighth title.

If not this year, then maybe next year, or the year after.

# Bibliography

Arnold, Peter. *Snooker Today*. London: Hamlyn, 1987.

Byrne, Robert, ed. *Byrne's Book of Great Pool Stories*. San Diego: Harcourt Brace, 1978.

Coover, Robert. *The Universal Baseball Association, Inc., J. Henry Waugh, Prop*. New York: Plume, 1971.

Davis, Joe. *How I Play Snooker*. London: Country Life, 1949.

Egan, Pierce. *Boxiana, or, Sketches of Ancient and Modern Pugilism*. London: G. Smeeton, 1812.

Everton, Clive. *The Embassy Book of World Snooker*. London: Bloomsbury Publications, 1993.

Everton, Clive. *Guinness Snooker: The Records*. Guinness, 1985.

Exley, Frederick. *A Fan's Notes*. New York: Vintage, 1988.

Fenichell, Stephen. *Plastic: The Making of a Synthetic Century*. New York: HarperBusiness, 1997.

Ford, John. *Prizefighting: The Age of Regency Boximania*. Newton Abbot: David & Charles, 1971.

Ford, Richard. *The Sportswriter*. New York: Vintage, 1995.

Holland, Jane. *Kissing the Pink*. London: Sceptre, 1999.

Lardner, Ring. *You Know Me Al*. New York: Scribner, 1991.

Oates, Joyce Carol. *On Boxing*. New York: Ecco Press, 1994.

Postal, Bernard, Jesse Silver, and Roy Silver. *The Encyclopedia of Jews in Sport*. New York: Bloch Publishing, 1965.

Stein, Victor, and Paul Rubino. *The Billiard Encyclopedia: An Illustrated History of the Sport*. Minneapolis: Blue Book Publications, Inc., 1994.

Thorburn, Cliff, and Clive Everton. *Playing for Keeps*. Haywards Heath: Partridge Press, 1987.

Trelford, Donald. *Snookered*. London: Faber & Faber, 1986.

Updike, John. *Golf Dreams: Writings on Golf*. New York: Knopf, 1996.

# Index